Rebel Folklore

Rebel Folklore

Empowering Tales of Spirits,
Witches and Other Misfits,
from Anansi to Baba Yaga

WRITTEN BY
ICY SEDGWICK

ILLUSTRATED BY
MELISSA JARRAM

Contents

6

The stories shared here represent a variety of communities, traditions, and beliefs passed down through families and loved ones. What we learn and take away from folklore is down to us and often our personal or communal interpretations. From identifying with struggles, to acknowledging powerful symbolism behind figures in folklore, stories like these help us to understand ourselves and the lives of others.

For me, folklore is a connection to our past and our ancestors; an anchor in a world where connection is going increasingly astray or sought through screens. There is a need to stop and truly listen, to put our phones down, to talk to one another, to connect with family and tradition. The passing down of stories is integral to our communities and in connecting with one another, no matter who we are or where we live.

I have always loved magical tales, and my obsession with mermaids and hidden underwater kingdoms started as a child, eventually leading me to write *Skin of the Sea*. But while I have long been captivated by stories of a different world under the waves, I never saw myself in these tales. Writing *Skin of the Sea* gave me the opportunity to address this and a way to deepen my connection with my father's Nigerian ancestry and folktales.

I have loved mermaids since I was six years old. These otherworldly beings with an affinity for water, saving or serving retribution, resonate with me in so many ways and hold an energy that has fascinated me. Melusina (see page 56), Yemanjá (page 176), Mami Wata (page 162), and the selkies (page 32) are all figures who wield divine power. The similarities of their courage, and sometimes vengeance, show the theme of feminine strength across multiple cultures.

When researching Mami Wata and Yemoja for *Skin of the Sea*, I was intrigued by the origins and beliefs of Black mermaids. For some in West Africa, Mami Wata was a warning for children not to go near deep water, not dissimilar to Jenny Greenteeth (page 22), the grindylow, and Peg Powler in England. In the Ifá spiritual belief system, Yemoja is a deity goddess who was said to have had a hand in creating the world. Those who were enslaved and forcibly taken to the Americas say that she offered comfort while others say she wrecked the slave ships.

Across the African diaspora, stories differ. Tales of Black mermaids have been passed down from generation to generation, village to village and country to country. Often keeping similar names, from Yemoja to Yemaya and Yemanjá, tales of these half-women half-fish were carried with them by Africans enslaved by Europeans. Representation of these magical Black women always include themes of nurturing, protecting, and exuding strength no matter what country. *Rebel Folklore* illuminates the connections of Black mermaids and the different beliefs of them from Africa to the Caribbean and South America.

Stories are constantly evolving and transforming. Anansi (page 150) is one such example of travelling folklore. Used to pass on information and advice, the spider god originated in Ghana with tales of him carried to North America and the Caribbean with the transatlantic slave trade. Much like the Black mermaids in *Skin of the Sea*, Anansi is a symbol of hope and resistance. Today, his stories live on as legend, even making appearances in various forms of pop culture.

Seeing the versions of psychopomps in this collection cements the importance we give to the journey after life. Ankou (page 58), found in Brittany, northern France, and Welsh folklore shares the skeletal features of the Grim Reaper that most of us are familiar with, but I was excited to see Meng Po (page 122), the goddess of forgetfulness in Diyu, the Chinese underworld. Much like Yemoja in my book, Meng Po helps those forget their memories of hell in preparation for reincarnation. It was thought-provoking to see the similarities to *Skin of the Sea* where Yemoja wipes the memories of Mami Wata in order to spare them the horrors of what happened when they were enslaved, as well as to prepare them for gathering the souls of others.

Shared through word of mouth, folklore opens worlds and keeps memories, customs, beliefs, and histories alive. *Rebel Folklore* is a dynamic collection of global figures that give us insight into many cultures from around the world. I hope you enjoy reading it as much as I did.

Natasha Bowen

At the root of the word 'rebel' is 'bellum': the Latin for 'war.' To 'rebel' is to make war and to be 'a rebel' is to be a warrior. *Rebel Folklore* is, by its very title, a battle cry for stories. But why bother? War is real and stories are not, surely? How could they have any power in relation to such real, terrifying threats as, say, a B61-12 nuclear bomb?

In my work with medieval European myths and legends, I have long been interested in how those tales of the past (often packed with prophecy and magic) were used to justify war. Warlords of the traditional, detonator-thumbing kind are storytellers as well as fighters. That will be true for as long as we humans endure. But the kinds of stories that feed wars are not like the ones you're about to read. The characters at their heart are 'glorious' paragons of physical and political might. You won't find many of those in the pages to come. Oh no. Not many of those at all.

The beings you are about to meet would be of little use in mobilizing a population against its neighbor. In fact, they would whoop, cackle, and snort at such an idea. But they will tell you what it is to dread your toddler falling in a weed-mantled pond. They will tell you what it feels like to long to give in to sexual desire, even if you know that you will lose many things you cherish if you do. And they will root down to the core of our yearning to be a little less fragile.

The beings you are about to meet reflect universal archetypes. Huayramama of Peruvian lore (see page 180) may be a great boa constrictor with the head of an old woman, but she is also a gatekeeper of the forces that dictate our lives (and which she might let us influence, if we promise to do good). The selkie, whose sexual allure is irresistible, must always go to the sea, and so personifies the bittersweet ephemerality, even the dangers, of desire. These stories and their characters are about huge, human issues like power, illness, hope, love, sex, and danger. It gives them inexhaustible force.

But, for all their universality, these beings are outcasts, mischief makers, threats to human society, as well as external guardians of it. They do not stand at the center with a sword in their hand. Nigeria's diminutive Zankallala (page 166), with bees swarming about his head and his serpentine staff, rides a scampering desert jerboa. The verdant grin of Jenny Greenteeth blends with the weeds in her watery lair. On Christmas Eve, Grýla (page 38) sits in her Icelandic cave, surrounded by the 13 capering Yule Lads (not to mention her Yule Cat) and stirs a stew made of naughty children. Meng Po waits at the exit of the Chinese underworld, with a bowl of forgetfulness soup. These characters and the stories we tell about them reveal the complexity of the human experience, rooted in places and cultures equally diverse.

Which leads me the central concern of this book: the relationship between ancient stories and life in the modern world. The first thing you will notice—the thing that probably got you picking it up off the pile in the bookshop—is Melissa Kitty Jarram's eye-spinning imagery. Her art pays homage to old iconographies (see Robin Hood, page 18), while glorying in a riotous, bare-breasted, fang-toothed-priestess palette of forms and vivid colors that is all contemporary. Be seduced. It's a fitting portal to the prose.

When you do start to read, you'll find Icy Sedgwick to be a sage and economical narrator. She introduces each character, tells a captivating story or two, then highlights themes ranging from the climate crisis to gender identity. She demonstrates that these old tales are not only delightful (or, sometimes, delightfully horrible), but also steeped in wisdom.

And what are we to do about that? First, we are to enjoy them. The world needs more delight. Second, we might even pick up our pens, brushes and laptops or put on our dance shoes and make something new. Each of these stories is a thousand potential stories. Whether we take our inspiration from the specific, archetypal, or a mixture of both, whether we learn all we can about Diyu and set our tale there or transplant a spider trickster (see Ghana's Anansi) into the modern digital realm, we have an opportunity to engage.

But that's not always easy. So often, when we decide to be 'creative', we think we need to be 'original'. But invention once came of putting both hands into your inventory and imaginatively recombining what you lifted out. *Rebel Folklore* is an inventory. Read it, observe it, absorb it, and delight in it. Then, if you feel like it, respond to it. To make art born of wonder defies the darkest threats of war. And today's stories are tomorrow's lore.

Amy Jeffs

11

Introduction

Storytelling is perhaps one of humanity's most enduring activities. Whether whispered in hushed tones around a fire, in a cosy tavern, or captured in writing to fix the tale like a fly in amber, we love to tell each other stories. And thanks to the boom in technology in the 20th century, stories are everywhere—and have never been easier to share. In such an environment, the renewed interest in folklore seems almost inevitable.

So what is folklore? At its heart, folklore refers to the knowledge, practices, and stories of 'the folk', i.e. people like you and me. These aren't the highbrow histories of powerful men and women in some distant corner of the past but, rather, the ideas, recipes, songs, and tales passed on from one person to another. Popular sayings, like "red sky at night, sailor's delight, red sky in the morning, sailor's warning," are examples of folklore. But it also includes your family traditions, passed on through generations, the seasonal events in your hometown, and the local figures that haunt the highways and byways of the area in which you live. Folklore, put simply, is alive, always evolving with some tales fading into obscurity, and new stories emerging to take their place.

Make no mistake, folklore is not necessarily 'true', but rather it preserves what people consider important. Some folklore is more relevant for a particular period, where it is shaped and honed by the lived experience of the people that used it. Other folklore lays bare the preoccupations of our ancestors, such as death omens. These omens were a way for people to feel a degree of control over lives that may often have felt at the mercy of the elements, animals, and other people.

Within this lore we find wonderful characters, often larger than life, sometimes loud enough to resound through the passing years, and at other times flexible enough to appear in different guises across our legends, landscape, and popular culture. Just look at Robin Hood, who continues to fascinate in his many incarnations, adaptations, retellings, and readings. These characters, these rebels, lay bare the shades of grey in life.

Nothing is truly black or white, and many
of these figures are neither entirely bad, nor
entirely good. Even those that may at first appear to be
villains, lurking in remote places to snatch the unwary,
often act as guardians for lonely locales, or they offer
cautionary tales to keep a community safe.

It's important for us to read these tales with their original contexts
in mind, to preserve the nuance of the stories but also to honor the
cultures that considered them valuable. Look at the Cihuateteo (see page
82); their importance to the Aztec civilization, and the fact that they
honored those who died in childbirth as warriors, tells us so much about the
respect they had for the physical act of birth. This is part of the beauty of folklore:
its ability to capture what people held dear or feared, transmitting them across the
ages through storytelling. The tales often contain key lessons, insights into human
psychology, and warnings to the unwary.

These aren't the highbrow histories of powerful men and women in some distant corner of the past, but, rather, the ideas, recipes, songs, and tales passed on from one person to another.

It is here that we find the value of folklore for teaching modern lessons. Imagine the
changes we could make if we took our lead from the Cihuateteo, and improved
maternity services across the world? Or how about taking a page out of Papa Bois's
book (page 92), and never taking more resources from the natural world than we

need? Think of the difference we could make to end-of-life care if we learned from the psychopomps—that people just want to understand what will happen to them?

There is, of course, a danger in reading tales from other, and older, cultures with a 21st-century Western mindset if we try to impose our values onto other stories. (Grýla is a strong, dominant woman but it would be a stretch to call her a feminist icon.) But if we read them with their context in mind, we can find universal themes that speak to a shared humanity: the forest protectors like La Madre Monte (page 182), Papa Bois, and Muma Pădurii (page 46) are still relevant today, while tricksters like Anansi and Zankallala teach us how to survive in a world where we may have less power than others. A surprising number of tales from across the world see predatory men seeking to steal the animal skins of shapeshifting women to force them into unwanted marriages, reflecting the misogynistic treatment of women, femmes, and girls the world over.

The tales often contain key lessons, insights into human psychology, and warnings to the unwary.

Consider these tales as introductions to 50 fascinating figures from folklore. Each profile provides an overview, examples of their stories, and an exploration of their continuing value in the 21st century. The profiles are a way to start a conversation with each figure, so if one of them speaks to your heart, seek them out, and learn more about them from their culture of origin. The wonderful illustrations throughout this book are interpretative, based on the myriad of versions of each story rather than traditional portrayals. Many of these characters have no definitive version thanks to the fluid nature of folklore, but hopefully they will help you encounter these figures in a different form. There are far more figures within folklore around the world than we could ever include here, so you'll also find a list of recommended reading and listening with which to further explore, via experts, storytellers, and folklorists (see page 186). But let's get started with these remarkable rebels. Perhaps these figures will mirror your own struggles, desires, ambitions, and victories. If they don't, they may still offer advice to help you get where you want to go...

CHAPTER 1

EUROPE

Robin Hood

Something rustles in the branches above, and the trees part long enough for you to catch a glimpse of Lincoln green among the leaves. Moments later, an arrow flies through the air, thumping into a wanted poster tacked to the tree behind you. You look at the face on the poster and laugh; you'd recognize that crooked grin and cheeky wink anywhere. Only Robin Hood could command that level of reward.

Robin Hood is one of the most famous rebels in literature, and he appears in English legends as an outlaw that lived in Sherwood Forest near Nottingham, UK. In some stories, he was made a fugitive for killing a deer, but he hid from the law in the forest with his fellow outlaws, the so-called Merry Men. Most famously, they targeted the Sheriff of Nottingham, wealthy landowners and other authority figures, distributing what they stole to the poor.

Robin Hood first appears in literature in 1377, and some versions of the legend claim he was a member of the nobility, Robin of Loxley. He's most often associated with Sherwood Forest, although other stories have him engaged in an archery contest with Little John in Whitby, Yorkshire. It's possible that the situation of his legend during the reign of Richard I is an 18th-century invention and there is little evidence to suggest he even existed. His original ballads date to the medieval period, although new ballads emerged in the 16th century, including those that introduced Maid Marian. Unlike many of the supernatural and mythical rebels in this volume, Robin Hood gets a death scene, and people still look for his grave even now. Surprisingly, the legends agree on his death, which happened after he fell ill and went to Kirklees Priory near Huddersfield. The prioress was his aunt and while she was supposed to nurse him back to health, she bled him to death to satisfy a villainous knight. Robin apparently fired a last arrow from his deathbed, and he's said to be buried where it landed. By this point, the true identity of Robin Hood almost doesn't matter, since his stories have been told and retold so often that he has taken on truly mythical status.

Perhaps the most obvious way in which Robin remains relevant is his status as a social justice warrior. His famous maxim, robbing the rich to feed the poor, highlights the imbalance of wealth between Robin's opponents and the poorest classes in Nottingham, and it's unforgivable that this imbalance continues in the 21st century. It's likely that laws restricting hunting (something the poor relied on to supplement

their meagre diets) inspired some of the first Robin Hood stories. *Encyclopedia Britannica* points out that the original ballads about Robin reflect the turbulence of the 14th century, which lead to the Peasants' Revolt. Robin became a symbol of the desire of ordinary people to stand up to authority.

The bond shared by Robin and his Merry Men is an interesting example of close male friendship that challenges stereotypes of gender and masculinity.

He also occupies the criminal underclass as an outlaw. Being an outlaw meant you didn't enjoy the protection of the law after you'd broken it yourself and avoided punishment. Even today, where we're still battling issues of police brutality and institutional racism, it's clear that living within the confines of the law doesn't guarantee it'll protect you, and this could also point to Robin's enduring popularity. He makes his own code of honor that protects those who are unprotected by the legal system.

We can also see Robin as a prototype environmental protector. While he and his Merry Men live in Sherwood Forest as it allows them to evade capture, their protection of the woods also turns them into guardians of the forest. They live off resources available within the woods, yet never appear to take more than they actually need, which shows an ability to live with the land rather than dominate it. We see such valuable practices among Indigenous cultures around the world, and while Robin isn't depicted as actively living in this way, this aspect of his lifestyle is often overlooked.

There have been queer readings of Robin Hood, suggesting that his close relationship with his Merry Men might be a metaphor for same-sex love. Certainly, the fact that Robin and his men live as outcasts on the fringes of society would chime with the experiences of ostracized queer men throughout history. Robin Hood is respectful towards women in the stories, and his band of Merry Men don't seem to be plagued by the same toxic masculinity that we see in some groups of men now (especially online). Though it's difficult to attach any labels to Robin Hood, since our understanding of sexuality has moved on so much in the hundreds of years since the tales were first told, the bond shared by Robin and his Merry Men is an interesting example of close male friendship that challenges stereotypes of gender and masculinity.

It's unsurprising that Robin Hood has made such an impact on popular culture. He's been a film and television favorite, not to mention the star of countless novels—all on top of the original ballads. Douglas Fairbanks, Sean Connery, Kevin Costner, Russell Crowe, and Taron Egerton have all played Robin Hood in film adaptations, and even Disney crafted their own version of the character in 1973, portraying Robin as a wily fox in his tangles with a big bad wolf (the Sheriff) and a cowardly lion (Prince John). The sheer number of variations—including BBC's *Maid Marian and her Merry Men*, which saw Marian as the true hero and Robin as a useless sidekick—shows just how flexible the legends of Robin are. This is Robin's greatest superpower— his ability to be exactly what we need him to be at that moment in time.

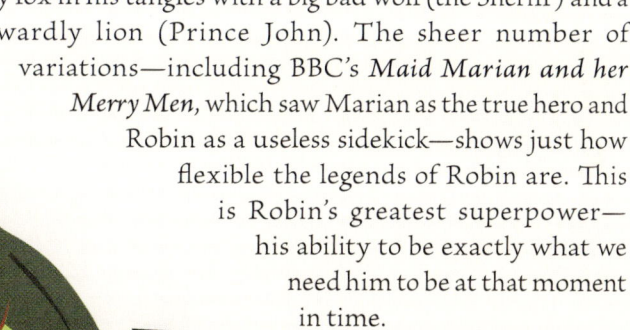

Jenny Greenteeth

A river burbles through a country park. Without warning, a haggard woman, with twigs caught in her knotted green hair and river slime clinging to her pale skin, lunges out of the water at a crow. She bares her sharp fangs and screeches. Jenny Greenteeth sinks back into the water, the duckweed closing over her terrible head.

Stories of Jenny Greenteeth still exist in living memory in Merseyside and Lancashire, in the northwest of the UK, with childhood warnings ringing in the ears of older residents. Jenny lurked among the duckweed-choked canals and ponds, and she'd drag children into the water if they got too near. In some stories, she ate her victims after drowning them, leaving no trace. In parts of Lancashire, hers is an alternative name given to duckweed, a dangerous aquatic plant that grows so dense it looks like grass, only to swallow the unwary person who tries to step on it.

In some stories, Jenny Greenteeth was a witch who lived in Liverpool where her ghost haunts St James' Cemetery. She lurks beneath the surface of lonely water, ready to snatch anyone who enters her domain. Others think the real inspiration for Jenny Greenteeth was a poverty-stricken woman who lived near St James' Cemetery, notorious for her appalling dentistry, which gave rise to her nickname. The poverty-shaming of a vulnerable woman overlooks the social conditions that left her in such a state and shows that a cruel disgust of poverty has a long history.

Yet she's perhaps more famous in her incarnation as a water-based spirit intent on drowning and devouring children. Other aquatic spirits haunt the waterways of northern England, including the grindylows of Lancashire and Yorkshire and Peg Powler of the River Tees. The grindylow lurked in rivers, ponds and marshes where it would drag unsuspecting children into the deepest waters if they ventured into the shallows. Powler, meanwhile, was a green-haired hag that lured children into the Tees with a froth on the river's surface known as 'Peg Powler's suds'.

Regardless of the difference in the name, the grindylow and Peg Powler play the same function as Jenny—all of them serve as cautionary tales to keep children away from water, and particularly the duckweed floating on it. While Jenny is clearly a monster, she also serves this valuable purpose. After all, even in urban places, we can find pockets of dangerous nature that we can't tame.

The Cailleach

It is late autumn, and many of the trees are casting aside their golden leaves. A giantess strides across the land, leaving a blanket of snow in her wake. She strikes the earth with her staff, and ice blossoms with every impact. Winter swaddles the landscape following her visit, while storms cluster on the horizon, eagerly awaiting their turn to arrive.

This is the Cailleach, a powerful creator goddess associated with Irish, Scottish, and Manx mythology. Her name means 'old woman' or 'hag', and it appears in terms like 'cailleach feasa', meaning 'wise woman'. She shapes the seasons, and even the land, throwing up mountains with her hammer. She's a strong and fierce old woman, often considered a 'crone' as part of the 'maiden, mother, crone' life cycle made popular within modern paganism. In some stories, she has a single eye and bluish-grey skin.

In many legends, she's contrasted with Brìghde, the youthful summer goddess who walks across the land between 1 May and 1 November. Some stories see the Cailleach and Brìghde as the same goddess, simply changing form to mirror the changing seasons. Other tales see the Cailleach turn to stone on either 1 February or 1 May, only returning to life on 1 November.

In one legend from Scotland, she's linked with Tigh nam Bodach, a thatched stone hut in Glen Cailliche, Perthshire. The name means 'house of the old man', and during the summer months, a collection of stones sits outside. The tale explains that the Cailleach is the largest stone, with two other stones being her husband, the Bodach, and their daughter, Nighean. Centuries ago, the locals gave the family shelter. In a show of gratitude, the Cailleach blessed them with a fertile glen whenever they stayed there. She promised the locals that if they cared for the stones, the glen would remain prosperous. The locals built the hut and every 1 May, they placed the stones outside, overlooking the glen. They moved the stones back inside on 31 October. No one is sure when the ritual began, but it continues to this day.

Other stories associate the Cailleach with the harvest itself, and she challenges young men to reaping competitions that she always wins—at a cost to them, as her victory means the loss of their life. One young man wins the competition by thrusting iron

spikes into the ground that blunt her scythe. Unable to keep up, the Cailleach leaves, sparing the young man and his companions. Some versions of the tale see him given the idea by the Cailleach's daughter, who takes pity and strives to help him avoid an early death.

Tracing the provenance of the Cailleach is not easy and the stories sometimes contradict each other. To some, she is so old her myth has no beginning. To others, she comes from Norway, crafting the landscape with the rocks she carried. The earliest stories appear in Ireland before moving to Scotland. She appears to pre-date more 'famous' Celtic gods, such as the horse goddess Epona, and is associated more with the land itself than with other gods. For the poet and spiritual activist

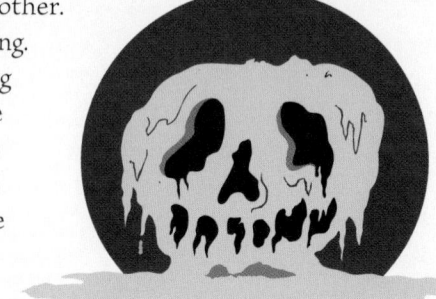

Patricia Monaghan, the Celtic goddesses of Irish mythology replaced the Cailleach, which perhaps explains why there are no holy places dedicated to her in the country.

In essence, the Cailleach represents female sovereignty, the wilderness, and the supreme power of nature.

The Cailleach has similarities with other seasonal tales, such as Persephone and Demeter in ancient Greece. The Persephone myth sees the goddess descend into the underworld to spend six months with Hades. Her mother Demeter misses her so much that she sends the world into autumn and winter. When Persephone re-emerges, the earth enjoys the return of spring. Such tales help to explain natural phenomena, although the Cailleach is far more forbidding than the maternal Demeter. She plunges the world into a harsh winter until Brìghde returns, and she's not always keen to hand the world over to her young counterpart.

In essence, the Cailleach represents female sovereignty, the wilderness, and the supreme power of nature. Some writers describe her as the personification of nature itself, which makes her a popular and valuable figure in the face of the climate crisis. Unlike many of the sanitized goddesses, recast as avatars of love or motherhood, the Cailleach is linked with the dangers of unpredictable weather. On the west coast of

Scotland, people believe she washes her plaid in the churning waters of the Gulf of Corryvreckan, an act that brings in winter. Her actions can look destructive, yet the quiet periods of rest enforced by winter are necessary for growth. She reminds us of the importance of winter to our agricultural cycles, something many of us no longer have contact with in the modern world.

The Cailleach is also a rare depiction of power associated with female old age in a world obsessed with temporary youth over the valid experience of the passing years. The Cailleach is ancient, but you would never call her elderly! She's often thought to have a healthy sexual appetite and several legends note she has outlived seven husbands. While their names are lost to history, hers is not. The opposition between the Cailleach and the youthful Brighde also shows that people preferring young women to their older counterparts is nothing new. Yet the cyclical nature of their eternal power share shows us how important both youth and age are: we cannot have one without the other.

Banshee

A woman sits on a tree stump at the edge of the abandoned forest, running a comb through her flowing silver hair. She keens as she combs, the mournful wail echoing among trees that stand as silent sentinels to her grief. Her eyes are red with sorrow and she cannot tell you why she cries, but you already know; the banshee only cries when someone dies.

The banshee is a famous figure from Irish folklore, also known as the bean sídhe, or 'fairy woman'. She announces an impending death with an impressive sorrowful cry, or she weeps and wails, a practice known as keening, for the loss. This keening would accompany the person's soul to the Otherworld.

The banshee was associated with a handful of clans, though which families are involved vary depending on the stories. If you heard her keening, you would know a member of your family would die the same night. In some tales, the banshee wasn't restricted to specific families and instead only appeared to those about to die in a violent way. She could comfort a murder victim's soul, but not warn them about what was to happen.

The stories vary as to the rules around the banshee's cry. In some parts of Ireland, people heard the cry for several nights in a row. In others, they heard her once, at the point the person died. People could hear the singing across great distances, but it only lasted a few minutes. If people heard several banshees at once, they knew someone powerful was about to die. If the family moved away, legend told that the banshee would go with them, which explains the banshee stories from America. Other versions claimed she'd stay behind at the family's home and cry at being left behind. Some think the banshee was an ancestor who continued to protect the family, which explained why she only keened for certain clans. Others say the banshee was a human woman who had suffered misfortunes and became a banshee following great sorrow, while yet more tales say she warns the family that death is near so they can prepare themselves.

In some tales, the banshee wears grey or white, her eyes are red from crying, and she has long, streaming silver hair. Some stories explain how she combs her hair, and that people wouldn't pick up combs they found in case the fairies kidnapped them. In other tales, she could take the form of hares, weasels, crows and stoats, all animals associated with witchcraft either because witches could take their form, or because witches kept them as familiars.

She could comfort a murder victim's soul, but not warn them about what was to happen.

There are accounts of banshee encounters in the National Folklore Collection at University College Dublin. In one, a student from Galway tells a story about a family in Ballinastack who had a banshee. One of the sons emigrated to America but fell ill soon after he arrived. The banshee followed the family back in Ireland as they did their work, crying all the while and, one night, a shadow passed by the door as they gathered by the fire. They later discovered this was the exact time the boy died in America.

Another story saw a guard from Kildare hear a banshee, only to be scoffed at when he told his replacement about it. The next day, the guard learned his replacement's father had died the day before, right at the same time that Patrick heard the wailing. A third poignant tale marked the arrival of Spanish flu in that part of Ireland in 1919. A woman heard a banshee while she was out gathering turf, and their neighbor, a Gallagher, fell ill with the flu the same night, only to die soon after.

The banshee may enjoy more rational origins, and some people think the wails are made by vixens or barn owls, both of which sound a little like a screaming woman. Certain legends have the wailing coming from woods near the afflicted home, so an animal origin for the cry is possible, although these don't explain how such sounds occurred at the specific time of death. Another explanation points to the keener, a

woman who sang sad songs at the graveside during funerals. People paid for the best singers and a person's greatness could be measured by how many mourners attended their funeral. A belief emerged that fairies sang at the gravesides of powerful families, since fairies were apparently better singers than humans. Over time, it's possible that these singing fairies became the banshee.

Unlike some singing spirits alledgedly dangerous to happen upon, such as Lorelei of the Rhine (see page 50), the banshee posed little threat to anyone who encountered her. After all, she had a job to do and no reason to get involved with anyone else. Yet the banshee seemed to dislike company and she would disappear if mortals appeared. If a person managed to catch her, they could force her to tell them exactly who would die. You would have to hope she didn't give your name!

The banshee is considered a sad figure as a harbinger of death, yet she doesn't cause anyone to die. She only announces it, ensuring that the person's life and death are marked and noticed. In this way, she holds space for mortality, and perhaps this is why she is so feared; not because she signals death, but because she reminds us of its continual presence in the background hum of our lives.

Selkie Folk

A sleek grey head pokes out of the water, sniffing the cold air. The seal hauls itself out onto the smooth beige sand and shrugs out of its skin to leave a woman, naked except for her long dark hair. The selkie neatly folds the skin and stows it under a nearby rock before dancing away along the beach.

Tales of the selkie appear most commonly in the Orkney Islands, off the coast of Scotland, but they also appear in the folklore of Ireland, the Faroe Islands, and Iceland. Selkies are shapeshifters, taking the form of seals in the sea and humans when they're on land. They shed their seal skin to reveal their human form beneath. If someone—usually a besotted and controlling man—steals their skin, then they must remain a human.

In many stories, human men steal the skins of female selkies, forcing them to become their wives. If the selkie finds her seal skin again, she'll regain her seal form and disappear into the waves. In other stories, the unsuspecting man knows nothing of his wife's true nature and will simply wake up one day to find her gone. Some stories see the selkies take their half-selkie children when they return to the sea; in others, they leave them behind, visiting them to play among the waves in their selkie form. The female selkie is often the victim of male power, a gentle creature that loves her children but misses her home. Anthropologist Allan Asbjørn Jøn points out that Hans Christian Andersen traveled in Scotland and may have heard the selkie tales, which could explain the relatively good nature of the mermaid in 'The Little Mermaid', compared to the vicious mermaids of folklore.

In the Orkney story of Goodman o' Wastness, a bachelor steals a selkie skin and forces the selkie to marry him. They have seven children together, but despite their apparent domestic bliss, she still looks for the skin whenever he leaves the house. One day, her seventh child tells her about the skin and the selkie reclaims it, returning to the sea and her selkie husband. Her human husband apparently spent much of his later life wandering on the beach, as if hoping for another glimpse of his selkie wife.

The Faroe Islands have a well-known selkie folk tale, the legend of Kópakonan, the 'seal woman', in which humans who killed themselves in the sea became seals. A local farmer stole Kópakonan's seal skin and forced her to marry him. Years later,

after bearing his children, she found her stolen skin and returned to the sea. The men of the village went seal hunting and killed the selkie's husband and sons, so Kópakonan cursed the men of the village to either fall from the cliffs or drown in the sea. The curse would only lift when there were enough dead souls to link hands around the island's edge.

A different selkie story from the Faroe Islands involves a human man who is caught in a vicious storm at sea. His selkie wife throws on her seal skin and saves his life, but because she has regained her seal form, she can never return to land; she saves his life, but she has to give up her human life in order to do so. This sad story at least suggests that some couples may have found happiness, even if the marriage began under dark circumstances.

The female selkie is often the victim of male power, a gentle creature that loves her children but misses her home.

Male selkies are less common, yet mischievous and less docile than their female counterparts. They appear as handsome men when they're humans, and in some tales, they romanced married human women and even carried them away. Women could summon male selkies by shedding seven tears into the sea, and the fact there's a charm to summon them shows that their presence was welcome. It's somewhat refreshing to see that women don't come to harm from the male selkie's amorous intentions, with them actively seeking out his company instead. It's possible that male selkies made a good excuse for dissatisfied wives to abandon their husbands!

In some stories, the selkies were the transformed souls of those who'd drowned at sea. In Shetland, the selkies come on land at midsummer to lure humans into the water, but as these humans don't return to the land, the implication is that they're drowned to become new selkies. Meanwhile, in the Orkney Islands, the stories differ, with some saying selkies could only become humans on Midsummer's Eve, and other tales saying they could do so every ninth night. Once they became humans, they danced on the shore in the moonlight or sunbathed during the day. They sound quite whimsical compared to other creatures of folklore.

For some scholars, the word 'selkie' comes from the Scottish word 'selich' (meaning 'seal'), though others think that the selkie might have arisen from a case of mistaken identity. Finnish or Sami women who married into Scottish families wore seal skins since they were waterproof, and seen from a distance, it might have looked like a seal removing its skin to reveal a human. There's also a slightly more sinister explanation since some believe the selkie story dates to earlier times, when health conditions were less understood. A clan in the Outer Hebrides had extra growths of skin between their fingers, something we would understand today as a genetic condition. Yet the clan claimed descent from intermarriage between the family and selkies to explain the resemblance of their hands to flippers. Much as we see within fairylore, where some scholars have wondered if changelings became a way for parents to explain away health conditions they didn't understand, selkies may have been a way for people to understand disabilities.

Pesta

An old woman, stooped with age and grim in her expression, shuffles along a jetty towards a waiting ship. She carries a rake in one hand, and an ancient tome in the other. One moment she stands on the jetty, the next moment she stands on deck. The ship eases away from the dock now that Pesta is back on board, and the locals can breathe a sigh of relief to see her leave.

In Norwegian legends, Pesta was an old woman who brought the plague with her, so people called her the 'plague hag'—an ageist term that emphasizes her talent for destruction. She carried either a rake or a broom; if she carried the rake, some would slip through its teeth and be spared the plague, but if she carried the broom, disease would sweep away everyone in her path. The legends also said she traveled from place to place on a rat-filled ghost ship, which makes some sense since it is widely believed that rats carried plague-ridden fleas from port to port on board boats. People thought the sailors on this ship were Pesta's earlier victims, now carriers of the plague.

While this may sound horrifying, and the rapid spread of fatal diseases is terrifying, Pesta does sometimes appear as fair and bound by a set of rules, which makes her actions feel less personal. In one folktale, Pesta hailed a boatman to carry her across a lake. During the journey, the boatman realized who she was. Fearing for his life, he asked her to let him live—even trying to strike a bargain that the journey would be free if she did so. Pesta consulted a mighty book she carried with her. After a few moments, she revealed that she couldn't spare him, but she would at least make his death easy. The boatman died in his sleep that same night; Pesta kept her word and held back his suffering.

Until the discovery of germs in 1861, people in Western societies looked to supernatural causes for illness, such as witchcraft, a punishment from God, or the arrival of a mythical creature. Personifying a natural phenomenon helped people to understand it, such as the Breton Ankou personifying death (see page 58). Such personification helped to explain something that people didn't understand, and the idea that the figure is just doing their job makes their actions more objective and less evil. They simply represent nature taking its course.

Grýla

A hideous old woman hunches over a vast cauldron, the light from the cooking fire throwing jagged shadows across the wall of the cave behind her. The sounds of hooves clatter on the stone floor as Grýla stirs the pot, chuckling to herself as she does so. A gigantic black cat sits nearby, gnawing on what looks suspiciously like a thigh bone.

Grýla is an ogress who lives in an Icelandic cave, leaving every Christmas Eve to steal the naughtiest children for her cooking pot. She hears whispers about misbehaving children throughout the year, and makes a Naughty List so she can gather them when she leaves her cave. She captures these badly-behaved children in her sack, before turning them into a stew. As the story goes, this less-than-appetising delicacy will last until the following winter.

Grýla doesn't live alone. She shares her home with the Yule Lads—13 mischievous trolls who play pranks in the days running up to Christmas—and her pet, the Yule Cat (or the Jólakötturinn). The Yule Cat has his own sculpture in Reykjavik and he has become famous outside Iceland in recent years, even starring in a short animation with music by Danny Elfman. The Yule Cat prowls Iceland on Christmas Eve and steals children who didn't get new clothes. This may sound shocking, but legend has it that those who finished their household chores before Christmas would receive new threads, and so it was implied that those who didn't finish their tasks had been too lazy. Being eaten by a giant cat made a great incentive to work harder!

Grýla's other companion is her third husband, Leppalúði (she killed the two that came before him, even eating the first). This mariticide underlines how grotesque Grýla is, and emphasizes her destructive power. Some writers think Grýla represents the wildness of nature, and her arrival in town marks the return of more primal forces in winter. She appears in 13th-century manuscripts, making her one of Iceland's oldest figures, and the message behind Grýla is similar to that of Santa—behave yourself and you'll be rewarded. While we might shudder at the extra brutality, it's possible this barbarism is derived from from the severity of Icelandic winters. The family needed to get everything done before the worst weather arrived, and not being eaten was good motivation for everyone to do their share. Seen in this light, Grýla becomes more of a cautionary tale than a punishing monster... as long as you remember she can hear you!

Baba Yaga

The trees rustle as something large bursts into the clearing. A giant mortar whizzes by, and an ugly old woman directs it with an oversized pestle. She cackles as she dives back into the forest, the trees crashing in her wake. You flee in the opposite direction to Baba Yaga, and pull up short when you see a wooden hut striding among the trees on giant chicken legs, the outside decorated with human heads.

Baba Yaga, the legendary figure of Russian folklore, has become quite the favorite of the online folklore community despite her complexity—or perhaps because of it. She appears as either an old woman or a trio of old women and even her name defies interpretation because, according to Baba Yaga scholar Andreas Johns, 'baba' can mean 'midwife' or 'sorceress' in Old Russian and 'grandmother' in modern Russian and Serbo-Croatian. 'Yaga' also proves tricky, since it could translate as anything from 'snake' to 'horror' to 'witch' to 'wicked wood nymph'.

She appears in folktales across Russia, Belarus, and Ukraine, although she was first mentioned in a book about Russian grammar from 1755. She even gets a fascinating origin story in a 1780 collection of Russian fairy tales, in which Vasilii Levshin explains the devil wanted to distil the essence of evil, so he put 12 horrible women into a cauldron and cooked them together, with Baba Yaga the end result.

Even though Baba Yaga is described as a witch, she prefers to fly in a mortar, wielding the pestle as a wand. She lives in a hut in the deepest, darkest parts of the woods, although you'd struggle to find her home—not because the directions are hard to follow, but because the hut walks around the forest on its massive chicken legs at Baba Yaga's whim. Baba Yaga doesn't live alone, keeping three servants who roam through the woods on horseback. The white rider represents the dawn, the red rider represents the sun, and the black rider represents the night, linking Baba Yaga with natural cycles of time. As they're her servants, it suggests she has command over the sun itself.

If you want to find the hut, and you'd have to be desperate to seek her help, you'd need someone to show you how to locate it. Many characters in the folktales get directions from magical threads, dolls, or feathers. Despite the terrifying hut, unconventional mode of transport, and fearsome reputation, people still sought Baba

Yaga's wisdom. She'd never offer help of her own accord, but if you asked then she might end up your best ally—as long as you successfully completed the tasks she set for you. This was a high stakes game: those who failed the tasks ended up in her cauldron as her next meal. But if a hero extracted a promise for help and managed to finish the tasks to her satisfaction? Then she kept her promise and provided the help they needed.

Perhaps the most famous story involving Baba Yaga is 'Vasilia the Beautiful', a Cinderella-like yarn that sees young Vasilia cast adrift when her mother dies and her father remarries. Her mother gives her a magical doll before she passes, but Vasilia is still stuck with an unpleasant stepmother and horrible stepsisters. When Vasilia's father leaves on business, his new wife sells their home and moves the family to a cottage in the woods. The bully stepmother gives Vasilia almost impossible tasks and, eventually, the stepsisters send Vasilia to Baba Yaga's hut in search of fire, counting on the witch's reputation for eating people.

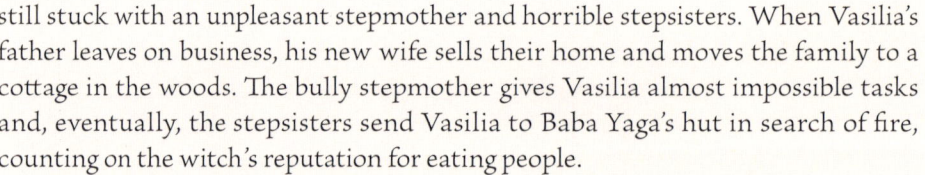
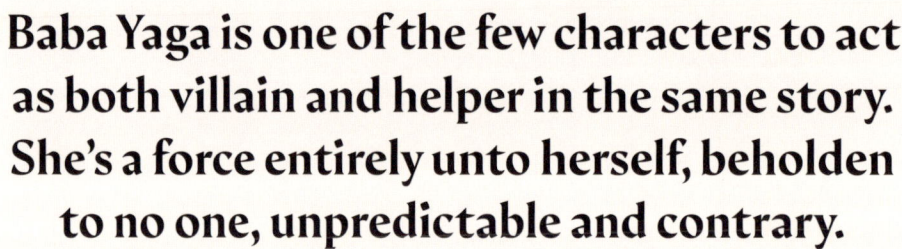

Baba Yaga is one of the few characters to act as both villain and helper in the same story. She's a force entirely unto herself, beholden to no one, unpredictable and contrary.

Unluckily for them, Baba Yaga isn't as predictable as they think, and she agrees to give Vasilia the fire she needs if she can finish a range of difficult chores. Baba Yaga is a far cry from the benevolent fairy godmother found in folktales, and she has no intention of making Vasilia's work easy. The tasks are hard, like separating wheat kernels from grains of rice under a time limit, but Vasilia's doll helps her to complete them in time. True to her word, Baba Yaga gives her the promised fire in a creepy lantern made from a skull and Vasilia heads home. The lantern incinerates her stepfamily when she returns, and Vasilia ends up marrying the Tsar of Russia, giving her a happy ending while rewarding her hard work at the hands of Baba Yaga. It's certainly one way to solve your dysfunctional family dynamic!

Early scholars looked for links between figures of folklore and ancient goddesses to see if these folk characters were deities hiding in plain sight in a new guise. Baba Yaga was one such figure, and a 1795 interpretation even linked Baba Yaga with Persephone, the Greek goddess of death and queen of the underworld. In the 19th century, Russian folklorists inspired by the Brothers Grimm and their German folklore project followed her appearances through European folktales to find a common thread. They found that time and time again, she comes to embody storms, winter, and death.

Baba Yaga has become an inspirational figure for many since she's so difficult to characterize. She can help the hero if she chooses to, giving her a degree of power and agency often denied to other female characters, but her aid comes with a price. Baba Yaga can also act as both the villain and trickster, harming or hindering a hero who strays into her path. In some stories, she's all these things at once, and her unpredictability makes her unique in European folklore. Other characters tend to work in a binary way, either helping or harming the hero, and while many of the characters in this volume are ambiguous, few are quite as wilfully individual as Baba Yaga. Russian folklorist Vladimir Propp divided characters from folklore into common roles, such as the hero, the helper, the villain, or the damsel needing rescue. Baba Yaga is one of the few characters to act as both villain and helper in the same story. She's a force entirely unto herself, beholden to no one, unpredictable and contrary. While we don't want to be the villain in our own lives, we can learn a lot from Baba Yaga's determined authenticity, ability to set (and keep) boundaries, and live life on her own terms.

Rusalka

A beautiful young woman dances naked on the grass beside a lake. Her flowing green hair falls around her shoulders as she sings, and she holds her hands up to the moon. The rusalka reaches the end of her song, giggles, and slips back into the water.

The rusalka is a water spirit, fond of seducing men and drowning them in rivers or lakes. These beings were once young women who became rusalki if someone drowned them, or they died by suicide in the water. Many blamed men for these unnecessary deaths, with unfaithful lovers, abusive husbands, and runaway bridegrooms the primary culprits. The murdered women lived as rusalki until the point at which they would have died naturally. Astrologer Sasha Ravitch notes a version of the tale in which a fairy rescues the doomed woman following her murder or suicide, turning her into a rusalka, with this transformation becoming both a curse and a gift of power.

For literature scholar Linda J Ivanits, the rusalki were the Russian counterparts of the Greek naiads, although northern rusalki were older and often unattractive, with long tangled hair and large breasts, while southern rusalki enjoyed beauty and youth. According to folklorist Vladimir Propp, before the 19th century the rusalka had a benevolent function. In the spring, they emerged from lakes to water crops as they passed, and women hung scarves and linen from trees as offerings. But by the 19th century, the rusalka was considered a dangerous ghost that haunted waterways. While the rusalki were no longer seen as helpful, most tales pointed out they weren't wholly evil. People feared the rusalka because she might lure young men into the water and drown them, but we could also view such an act as a preventative measure. The rusalki could save other young women by killing the type of young man who would look for a sexy rendezvous from a strange woman in a lake. A rusalka could die in peace if someone avenged her death, supporting the idea that she just wants justice.

It's not uncommon for the rusalki to help witches or abused women. Much like Mami Wata (see page 162), the rusalka might also take a favored lover to her underwater home, although mortal men could find themselves unable to meet the rusalka's insatiable appetite. Other men captured rusalki and baptized them, turning them into humans so the men could marry them, in a similar move to the men who forced selkies and bird women into marriage. Despite their murderous tendencies, the rusalka ultimately seeks to help other women while avenging her own death.

Muma Pădurii

A loud creak echoes around the forest, before something enormous crashes through the trees behind you. You freeze and make the sign of the cross with your fingers as you watch a giant woman stride past. Her tangled hair tumbles down her back and brushes along the forest floor, and she pushes branches aside with hands that look like the gnarled, bony fingers of a fairytale witch. That's almost what Muma Pădurii is, though she's far more ancient—and terrifying—than that. She glances down at you and nods once before disappearing into the depths of the forest.

Muma Pădurii's name means 'Mother of the Forest', though she's sometimes considered to be a forest spirit who takes the form of an old woman. Many of the stories emphasize her ugliness, describing her tangled hair and twisted hands, and she's believed to live in the depths of the woods in a hidden house. Descriptions vary, with some stories describing her teeth as stolen millstones, and others claiming her height to be over that of a fir tree. In one vivid image, her hair is made of snakes, reminiscent of the mighty Medusa of Greco-Roman myth. Elsewhere, she wears clothing made of leaves and can shift her form whenever she wants to, hinting at a similarity to Colombia's La Madre Monte (see page 182). The Muma Pădurii of Transylvania—where she is sometimes known as Valva—also lives in abandoned mines, and her attitude towards humans is nearly always negative.

The ugly crone version of Muma Pădurii hides from humans, but if anyone passes her home alone she might kill them, or drive them mad with fear. She'd sneak into houses at the edge of the woods to punish and kill whoever lived there, presumably for daring to set up a dwelling so close to her own. The descriptions of Muma Pădurii's house vary depending on the stories in which she appears. In some fairy tales, it is surrounded by a fence spiked with human heads, similar to the gory architectural choices of Baba Yaga in Russian lore (see page 40). Muma Pădurii could enchant young girls to act as her slaves around the house, or force young men to act as her servant for a year in exchange for one of the foals birthed by her magical mare.

Other stories describe her as a beautiful young woman masquerading as a benevolent fairy if she finds lost children in the woods. But she harbors only ill intentions, and will harm and even kill the lost children once she catches them. Women feared that Muma Pădurii might steal their infants or bring disease, so they would put scissors and a broom

beside the cradle to ward her off. This perhaps hints at her fairy-like nature, since people in the British Isles hung scissors above their child's cot to prevent fairies from stealing their children to swap them for changelings. This tradition, which today's health and safety regulations might balk at, came from a belief that the fairy folk couldn't stand iron. In some ways, Muma Pădurii comes to represent the fear of the unknown, especially in earlier times and rural areas, when peril was greater for small children. Muma Pădurii has children of her own with the Old Man of the Young Forest, and in some stories, she steals the sleep of any unprotected children to give this to her own offspring. Perhaps this helps to explain any sudden illness in young children or bouts of unexplained crying in healthy children who can't fall asleep.

Yet we can't see Muma Pădurii as being entirely evil. After all, she's the Mother of the Forest, and she cares for the animals and plants living in her domain. This perhaps explains why she lives where she does, in the very heart of the sylvan realm, since it places her as far removed from humans as possible. Living at the center of a primordial forest, she has a direct connection to nature at its most untouched. This also explains those stories in which she drives humans mad with fear because she sees them as trespassers on her land. In one story, if a man could succeed in capturing Muma Pădurii, then she had to grant him a wish. Similar stories appear in other countries, such as Scotland's Bean Nighe—capturing this death prophetess before she could see you forced her to grant you three wishes.

Damage to the trees or harm befalling the animals in the forest hurts this ancient forest spirit. Some very early legends see her helping people in trouble or punishing thieves that venture onto her lands. In some of these stories, she even helps lost children who stray into the forest, since they are as yet untouched by the greed and apathy that sees adults cut down trees with abandon. She may even see these children as victims of negligent adults and help them out of a sense of pity. This contradicts the later stories in which Muma Pădurii poses a danger to very young children, but contradictions often lie at the heart of folktales, since stories evolve to suit their location and the people telling them. Folktales often also change to suit new purposes, so recasting a nature spirit as a malicious witch might sever a community's links with its environment, making it much easier to plunder natural resources.

Recasting a nature spirit as a malicious witch might sever a community's links with its environment, making it much easier to plunder natural resources.

Professor and folklorist Claudia Costin describes Muma Pădurii as an example of one of several feminine monsters in Romanian folklore, though she stresses that these characters are always ambivalent. They can both help and harm humans, and they often represent justice or morals, something we can see in the legends of Muma Pădurii where she helps lost children and punishes loggers. Costin also suggests figures like Muma Pădurii act as a way to both explore a fear of the unknown and also to remember ancestors and ancient gods. In some regions, offering Muma Pădurii bread, or making the sign of the cross in her presence, could soothe her temper, perhaps through showing her generosity or deference. Her evolution from a respected nature spirit into a feared witch could suggest a change in our own behavior, with ancient deference for the dark places of the world replaced by greed for the resources these places provide. Muma Pădurii reminds us of our former relationship with nature, rather than our intended dominion over it.

Lorelei

A beautiful song fills the cool dusk. A cascade of perfect notes tumbles around you, like a scattering of diamonds and pearls in musical form. You look for their source and there, she sits on the edge of the cliff! The dying rays of the setting sun turn her hair the color of molten gold, and she runs a glittering comb through her luxurious tresses. Lorelei sings her haunting melody and though you can't make out the words, you know she sings of lost love, abandoned maidens, and ancient magic. The song ends while you hurry to reach her, and when you finally get to the top of the rock, only twilight awaits.

The Lorelei is a slate rock near Sankt Goarshausen in the Upper Middle Rhine Valley in Germany. It stands 132m (about 433ft) high and this part of the river is a UNESCO World Heritage Site, despite the number of river accidents involving the treacherous rocks below. But the name 'Lorelei' also refers to a water nymph, famous in local legend, and if you believe the stories, the locals named the rock after her. A bronze statue of Lorelei was erected as a memorial just below the Lorelei rock in 1983, which is still popular with tourists.

German writer Clemens Brentano collected the legend and immortalized it in print in 1801. In his version, Lorelei was a beautiful woman who lived in the area, and she waited on the clifftop for her knight lover to return whenever he went to war. One day, he didn't come back, and while Lorelei didn't know what had happened to him, she assumed he'd abandoned her in favor of another woman. She sang on the cliffs as a way to work through her sadness, but the locals didn't take kindly to her presence. They accused her of bewitching men with her beautiful singing voice, and Lorelei was sentenced to be burned at the stake for practising sorcery. The local bishop couldn't find it in him to have her executed, and he forgave her for her sins (those of simply singing on a clifftop). He sent the maiden to a nunnery, assuming that a life dedicated to Christ would help her to overcome her sadness. On the way there, Lorelei asked her knight chaperones if she could take a final look at the Rhine from the rock. She fell to her death, with some versions claiming she jumped because she thought she saw her knight on a boat in the river.

The story changed in 1824 when Heinrich Heine immortalized the nymph in his poem, 'Die Lorelei', in which he turned Lorelei into a dangerous enchantress. Rather

than singing forlornly for her lost love, this version of Lorelei deliberately lured sailors onto the rocks below with her voice. Heine used familiar imagery associated with mermaids, such as Lorelei's unsurpassed beauty and her habit of combing her hair while she sang. Where the previous maiden was wrongly accused of sorcery, this nymph went all out in her quest to drive ships to their doom.

In another version of the legend, a beautiful maiden was deeply in love with her partner. Unfortunately, he didn't take the relationship as seriously as she did, cheating on her time and again. His infidelity so wounded the maiden that she threw herself into the river. Her soul was so consumed by despair over her lover that she turned into a malicious water spirit, intent on destroying men by luring them onto the rocks as a form of revenge on her cheating partner.

The changing versions of the legend in the 19th century capture the only two models of femininity available to Victorian women— the angel of the hearth, represented by the forlorn maiden singing for her lost love, and the fallen woman.

Yet another version of the legend sees Lorelei again portrayed as a dangerous water nymph, enchanting sailors with her singing voice from her favorite spot on the rock. In this version, a monk named Goar arrived in the region and started converting the local pagans to Christianity. One of them told him all about Lorelei and the danger she posed to anyone trying to use the river. One day, Goar headed along to his favorite fishing spot by the river, where he found a naked woman sitting right where he always sat. Armed with the knowledge about Lorelei, Goar knew exactly who she was, though he was unafraid of this pagan water nymph. She tried her usual tricks on him, beckoning him towards her, but Goar was uninterested, and he banished her with a powerful speech. Having vanquished Lorelei, Goar later found it far easier to convert the locals.

Some think that the nymph's beautiful singing was actually the echo caused by the rock itself. Over time, different legends appeared to explain the acoustic phenomenon. Yet as with other folktales that seek to warn people of dangers around water, it's possible that the Lorelei rock gained its reputation precisely because it was so treacherous for boats. Knowledge of the rocks became encoded in the legends, which were memorable and easily passed on, and the stories fitted in with other tales of dangerous mermaids and the sirens of Greek myth, who lured men to their deaths with their haunting voices.

The changing versions of the legend in the 19th century capture the only two models of femininity available to Victorian women—the angel of the hearth, represented by the forlorn maiden singing for her lost love, and the fallen woman, associated with the dangerous nymph luring men to their deaths. One Lorelei is a victim of male behavior, while the other lashes out at men indiscriminately. While we can see the story as a metaphor for the dangers posed to men by their lust for women, it also reminds us of the constraints placed on female behavior. That said, the story also offers a third way, one embraced by Adele, Taylor Swift, and others—and that's to enjoy the therapeutic nature and creative power of music. Sing on, sister.

Moura

A small well stands in a picturesque square at the end of the village. Tourists pause to snap selfies and a figure suddenly shimmers into view, combing her long hair. The moura winks at you before disappearing from sight... for now.

The moura is often associated with wells, springs, and caves, although they're sometimes considered the builders of dolmens, hill forts, and megaliths, too. They're prodigiously strong, able to haul heavy stones, and they're also seductive shapeshifters, sometimes appearing as snakes. Ancient spells trap mouras at wells or springs, and these spells can only be broken by a kind human, so the moura offers fabulous treasure in exchange for her freedom.

In one tale, the moura appeared as a half-woman, half-snake creature. She offered a young man from the village unimaginable wealth if he would let her take her true form as a serpent and wrap herself around him. He agreed, perhaps not fully realizing what she was asking, and she transformed into a snake. The horrified youth struck the snake, and she slithered away, sobbing that he'd merely strengthened the enchantment upon her, and she was never seen again.

No single moura legend exists, since different Portuguese towns have their own versions, but common elements exist across the stories. The moura sings while combing her hair, although she might spin yarn or do washing. (She has this in common with fairy women found in Ireland, Scotland, and Wales, hinting at shared Celtic origins through the Celtic presence in the Galician region of Spain and their ties to Portugal.) The moura's link with the well, and the persistent hair-combing, also associates her with water spirits and mermaids, even if she isn't depicted as such.

In the 19th century, folklorist Oswald Crawfurd proposed that the word 'moura' referred to the Moorish culture that lived in the Iberian Peninsula, and that the moura was a Moorish maiden haunting each parish's well. In these stories, humans could only see the moura on St John's Day, 24 June, and some stories see young women coming to draw water from the well and hearing plaintive singing, even though they didn't see the moura. The mouras are mysterious, rather than dangerous, and they're often more at risk of harm from humans since human intervention can cause their entrapment to be extended.

Melusina

A narrow archway nestles beneath two houses in the Castello district of Venice, with a brick heart above the arch at one end. Legend has it that if you and your lover touch the brick heart together, your love will last forever.

The story begins when a young fisherman named Orio accidentally catches a mermaid named Melusina in his fishing net—an unlikely meet cute, but it marked the start of a budding romance. Orio proposed and Melusina agreed to give up her tail for human legs. She had one condition: Orio should never visit her on a Saturday until they were married. He kept his word for two weeks, but impatience got the better of him and, on the third Saturday, he headed to their meeting place. After waiting for several hours, a giant sea serpent reared out of the water.

Melusina had been cursed to become a snake every Saturday, but marrying Orio would break the spell. In love and prepared to look beyond this red flag, the couple married anyway. They had three children, and were happy until Melusina fell ill and died. Yet even after her death, someone kept caring for the children while Orio was fishing. One Saturday, he came home early and found a giant snake in the kitchen. He killed the serpent with an axe. After that, no one did the housework or cared for the children. Horrified, Orio realized that he had lost his wife for a second time.

The story has much in common with the 15th-century Mélusine myth from France. Like her Italian counterpart, Mélusine was victim to an unfortunate curse that saw her transform into a serpent from the waist down every Saturday. Generations later, some noble families claimed descent from Mélusine: having a powerful, protective ancestor was a great way to boost your image. Even now, some think the two-tailed Starbucks mermaid may be a reference to Mélusine.

Both stories feature women who become monstrous creatures as the result of a curse. They highlight the changing nature of the female body, perhaps rendered monstrous in the eyes of their husbands. It's possible this is a comment on the physical changes brought about by childbirth, while the weekly transformation could reference the monthly changes caused by menstruation—both changes that can confuse those not personally experiencing them. Melusina at least finds a loving companion in Orio, and it is his ability to see beyond her curse that allows him to break it.

Ankou

Something squeals in the road behind you and you leap to safety behind a parked car. A painfully thin white horse heaves a heavy wooden cart, and the bundles of rags it is loaded with shake with every rattling movement. The wheels screech as they bump over every rut and rock in the road, and a tall figure comes into view. He's immense; so tall you can't even put a figure on his height, and a wide-brimmed black hat casts his face in shadow. He wears a black robe, and the pale hand that grips the handle of a scythe is so bony it barely looks real. You squeeze your eyes closed and wait for Ankou to pass before you dash out of your hiding place.

Ankou is a psychopomp most commonly found in Breton folklore from northern France, although he does also appear in some Welsh, Anglo-Norman, and Cornish stories. The psychopomp appears in myths across cultures, time periods, and locations to collect the soul at the point of death and deliver them wherever they need to go. Two of the most common descriptions of Ankou see him as either a tall, thin man wearing a hooded cloak, or he appears as a skeleton wearing a broad-brimmed hat and carrying a scythe or an iron whip. Many stories emphasize his great height, made even more apparent by his extreme thinness, while long white hair falls in tangles down his back. To complete this image of desolation and impending death, emaciated horses pull his cart through the streets.

The skeleton, the hooded cloak and the scythe are all features of the Grim Reaper, and we're familiar with these depictions from popular culture—just look at Death in Terry Pratchett's *Discworld* books. The image of Death as a skeleton is an old (and obvious) one, dating back to 16th-century woodcuts in which a dancing skeleton becomes an embodiment of Death. Likewise, carvings and statues of Ankou appear on and inside churches around Brittany, and they often depict a skeleton clutching a scythe.

Unlike Death, who is often depicted as simply appearing before the person he's about to collect, Ankou might arrive at a house to collect the deceased soul, politely knocking on the door for admittance. In other stories, he stands wailing in the street outside the house to call the dead to the door, and elsewhere, he travels with one or two ghostly assistants who enter the house and lead the dead outside for collection by Ankou. Meeting Ankou while he was carrying out his duties was thought to be a bad omen and in the worst cases even caused your own death. Even hearing Ankou going about his business was best avoided. People feared hearing the squealing wheels of his wheelbarrow so much that even hearing train wheels screeching outside your home was thought to announce the passing of Ankou. The wailing of Ankou outside the house, or the squealing of the wheels on his cart, may also have an earthly origin, since Breton folklore also talks of a 'death bird' that cries near the house of someone who is about to die, most often thought to be an owl, a crow, or a magpie.

Each parish has its own Ankou, always taken from within the community, and Ankou served a further function of guarding the parish graveyard. This version of Ankou keeps death within the wider family of the community.

One of the earliest written stories about Ankou from the 19th century told the tale of a young man who heard his coach approaching. He'd always wanted to see Ankou for himself so he hid behind a hazel tree to watch Ankou pass. Sure enough, the coach rattled along the road, its axles squealing with the effort, and three white horses hauled it towards him. Two men wearing black walked alongside the coach, and the axle finally snapped when the coach drew level with the hazel trees. Ankou ordered one of his assistants to make a new one using one of the trees, and the young man sighed with relief when the assistant undertook his repairs but didn't seem to see him. But his escape was short-lived; the young man took ill as dawn began to break and died shortly after.

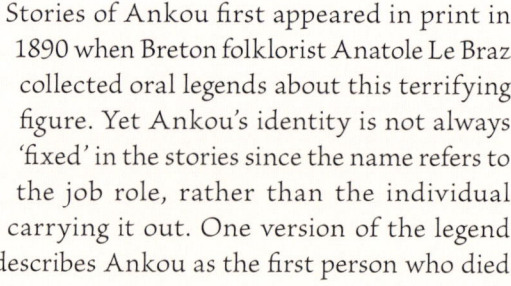

Stories of Ankou first appeared in print in 1890 when Breton folklorist Anatole Le Braz collected oral legends about this terrifying figure. Yet Ankou's identity is not always 'fixed' in the stories since the name refers to the job role, rather than the individual carrying it out. One version of the legend describes Ankou as the first person who died

in a new year, and that person collected the souls of the dead until the following year, when the role passed on. Having carried out a year in the role, the previous Ankou could retire into the afterlife, leaving their replacement to work for the rest of the year. An alternative version of this story sees Ankou as being the last person to die in a year, and they serve their term until the last death of the following year. In either of these explanations, each parish has its own Ankou, always taken from within the community, and Ankou served a further function of guarding the parish graveyard. This version of Ankou keeps death within the wider family of the community.

It is somewhat unusual that, even though folklore specifies that the Ankou is the person who died, the figure is referred to as 'he'. This is particularly strange given the proximity of women to death in earlier times, as those who would wash and prepare the body for burial, often sitting with the dead until they were taken to the churchyard. We could comment on gender roles or stereotypes, but it is possible that Ankou was simply the form the deceased took to carry out the task of collecting souls.

Korea's Jeoseung Saja (see page 112), Greece's Hermes, Egypt's Anubis, and animals and birds such as dogs, cats, ravens, and even seahorses also carry out the role of psychopomp in other religions and belief systems. Yet, by comparison, Ankou feels somewhat less remote, and somehow more familiar, due to their emergence from within the community. While Ankou is still a forbidding figure since they represent death, knowing that you once knew this psychopomp makes the transition to the afterlife somehow less clinical and more bearable through the warmth of community bonds.

CHAPTER 2

NORTH AMERICA

Loup-Garou

Your Uber pulls up outside your house and you climb out onto the pavement. Frost flavors the night air with hints of winter and you hurry up the path to your house, keen to get back into the warmth of home. As you unlock the front door, a noise across the street catches your attention and you look at the house opposite. Your neighbor slips out of their house, looks up and down the street, and turns into a wolf, his limbs popping and crackling into their new positions. He unleashes a single, bloodcurdling howl before bounding up the street.

Shapeshifting humans appear in cultures throughout time and around the world, including figures in this book, such as Brazil's boto encantado (page 170), the selkies of northern Europe (page 32), the Caribbean's Papa Bois (page 92), and the fearsome Arabic jinn (page 104). The Loup-Garou is a French creation often found in French Canada, and while it's mostly considered to be a werewolf, it can also appear as owls, horses, cats, dogs, pigs, or oxen. The transformation of the person into another form is often more important than the exact form that the person takes. Unlike traditional werewolves, who transform during the full moon, the Loup-Garou transforms every night. They roam outside in their animal form, though the stories are less bloodthirsty than those of European werewolves.

In French Canadian tales, humans could become the Loup-Garou if they neglected their Christian faith by failing to confess at Easter or working on a Sunday. A common thread in many stories was that the cursed person hadn't taken mass in seven years. The number seven is commonly found in folklore (think deadly sins, virtues, dwarves, seas, and so on), while not attending mass meant the person had broken the social contract by withdrawing from religious life.

Others became a Loup-Garou after selling their soul to the Devil. Those who did this would be forced to run in their animal form for 40 nights, at which point the Devil would claim you, although you could be freed from the curse if someone recognized you and drew your blood. This ability to be freed from the curse sets the Loup-Garou apart from werewolves, which famously need to be dispatched with silver bullets. But if a person recognized the Loup-Garou while they were in their animal form, and managed to draw blood from them, it broke the curse and returned them to their human state, on the condition that neither of them ever spoke of it.

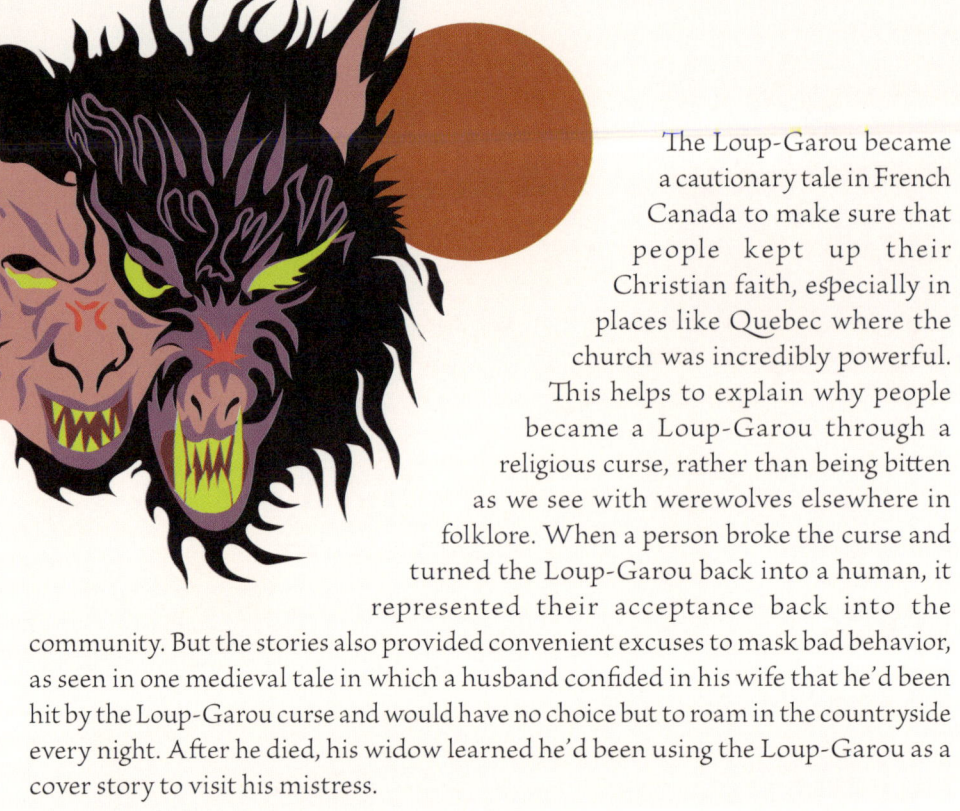

The Loup-Garou became a cautionary tale in French Canada to make sure that people kept up their Christian faith, especially in places like Quebec where the church was incredibly powerful. This helps to explain why people became a Loup-Garou through a religious curse, rather than being bitten as we see with werewolves elsewhere in folklore. When a person broke the curse and turned the Loup-Garou back into a human, it represented their acceptance back into the community. But the stories also provided convenient excuses to mask bad behavior, as seen in one medieval tale in which a husband confided in his wife that he'd been hit by the Loup-Garou curse and would have no choice but to roam in the countryside every night. After he died, his widow learned he'd been using the Loup-Garou as a cover story to visit his mistress.

When a person broke the curse and turned the Loup-Garou back into a human, it represented their acceptance back into the community.

The French controlled vast swathes of North America in the 17th century, including Quebec in Canada and New Orleans in the United States. They naturally brought their legends and traditions from France, including the Loup-Garou, and the presence of the French in Haiti in the 17th century helps to explain the presence of Loup-Garou legends there as well. Here, the term refers to spirit-possessed people who transform into animals to drink the blood of children. Following the devastating earthquake in 2010 that hit Haiti's capital, Port-au-Prince, a man was accused of being a Loup-Garou after he was caught abducting children amid the chaos.

More famously, the Loup-Garou also appears in French Louisiana, where it is called the rougarou, and it's believed to prowl the swamps around New Orleans. Some people have described the rougarou as being a human with a dog's head. Much like its French Canadian cousin, the rougarou became a punishment for anyone breaking Catholic traditions. The rougarou sometimes provides a boogeyman so parents can cajole children into behaving—the rougarou will come for them if they don't. It also made a great reason to avoid the woods at night. Elsewhere, the rougarou hunts Catholics who don't fast for Lent, though it's not recommended that you try to free the rougarou from its curse. If you draw its blood, you break the curse for the rougarou but it transfers to you.

A whole range of climate issues, including hurricanes and rising sea levels, have impacted Louisiana's coastline, and rougarou tales began to disappear along with its favored habitat. Rougarou Fest launched in 2011 to raise funds for the wetland areas, and people dress up as different interpretations of the rougarou. This rehabilitation of the rougarou has both raised its profile and helped draw attention to the effects of climate change. Where the rougarou once punished people for neglecting their religious commitments, it now symbolizes habitat loss, and the damage caused by neglecting environmental concerns. This is one curse that we need to break together.

Bell Witch

A cave yawns in the hillside, its rock walls wet with moisture. The atmosphere feels strange, somehow stiff, and the hairs on the back of your neck stand up. A voice whispers something indistinct in your ear, though there is no one else near the cave but you. It tells you its name, though the Bell Witch needs no introduction, before the presence melts away into the shadows.

The Bell Witch case is often considered to be America's most documented ghost story, and it's certainly one of the most famous. Much of the existing discussion emphasizes the Bell family at the heart of the tale, who were plagued by an unseen presence in their Tennessee home between 1817 and 1821. The entity that became known as the Bell Witch physically assaulted family members, while a mysterious voice verbally tormented them. According to legend, the spirit even accompanied the youngest daughter, Betsy, to the houses of other people, reminding her it could follow her anywhere. The death of the family patriarch John is even blamed on the spirit. The ghost is still often associated with the Bell Witch Cave, some 40 minutes by car from Nashville.

But who was the Bell Witch?

The most popular version of the story is that the Bell Witch was the ghost of Kate Batts, one of the family's neighbors who looked on the Bells with an unkind eye after a land purchase turned sour. The disembodied voice claimed that it belonged to a disturbed spirit, a spirit of someone buried in the nearby woods, and even an ancient spirit that came "from everywhere." Whatever the truth, the spirit enjoyed performing unusual party tricks, such as reciting sermons that were given 12 miles apart at the same time. She apparently had power over animals, causing horses to stop in their tracks and refuse to move. This recalls English fairy lore, in which fairies might enchant farm animals; only the sunrise, or touching the bewitched beasts with a rowan branch, would break the spell.

The reports of physical harm at the hands of the Witch suggests the arrival of a poltergeist on the farm. These noisy ghosts appear in folklore to explain disappearing objects, unexplained sounds, and physical injuries, and in parapsychology circles they're usually associated with teenage girls—Betsy Bell was 11 when the haunting began. Experts are undecided whether poltergeists are the spirits of the dead, or a separate entity entirely, and there is a crossover between the poltergeist and various house spirits in folklore such as brownies. In European folklore, brownies would tidy a messy home and throw a tidy home into disarray. Leaving dishes of cream or honey cakes showed your appreciation for the brownies, helping them to be well-disposed towards you, though leaving a gift of clothing would offend them and cause them to leave. Perhaps the Bell family neglected such customs and insulted their invisible house guest.

The agency she wielded in a time of general female powerlessness would have made her a threatening figure.

Much of the discussion about the Bell Witch focuses on the damage she caused to both people and property, such as the welts left on Betsy's body. Yet the spirit also cared for the Bell family matriarch Lucy when she was ill and engaged in lengthy chats with one of the family's sons, John Junior. This tendency towards favoring individual members of the family adds a layer of ambiguity to the story since the spirit is by turn benevolent and vicious, depending on its whims. Such favoritism also suggests intelligence at work, something that makes a poltergeist less likely, since they're not famous for their conversational abilities—though it could still suggest fairy activity. In folklore, fairies can be ruthless towards those who disturb, maim, or otherwise alter their land without permission, which brings a whole new interpretation to the claim that the spirit came from the woods. That the Witch promised to return in seven years, a common time span within folklore and fairy tales, is also a telling detail.

In past centuries, desperate people might turn to witchcraft if they felt official channels were closed to them, choosing to use magic to find lost items, settle disputes, and gain a sense of power in a world that otherwise removed their rights and opportunities. But little of the Bell Witch's activity is in keeping with the witchcraft of lore and horror stories. She discussed Christianity with John Jr, quoted scripture, and pottered around the farm without a broomstick or cauldron in sight. The label 'witch' wasn't just hurled at those suspected of practising actual witchcraft, though; it was also an insult, thrown at a disliked member of the community to discredit and ostracize them. The Bell Witch clearly had a hearty appreciation for her own power, and the agency she wielded in a time of general female powerlessness would have made her a threatening figure.

The Bell Witch has become a folklore legend in her own right and continues to fascinate people two centuries after the events on the Tennessee farm. The mystery will remain unsolved and fans of the case can only speculate about the Witch's true identity. Though in some ways, the Witch's identity is beside the point. This story contains elements from a variety of folklore, and the resultant blend is both unusual and symptomatic of the slippage between different strands of lore. Any crossover between fairies and ghosts shows just how ambiguous both types of entities are, showing us how flexible folklore can really be, while the Witch becomes an unexpected symbol of female might, apparently from beyond the grave.

Seven Sisters

A beautiful Black woman, resplendent in royal blue, sits before you. After a few moments, she proclaims your future and you leave her reading room. Out in the main shop, you see her standing behind the counter... only now, she wears fiery orange. She nods at you and you nod back, thoroughly confused. How did she get changed so fast? You move to leave and look back into the shop. The woman now stands outside the reading room, clad in canary yellow.

According to legend, the Seven Sisters of New Orleans worked in the Crescent City in the 1920s, sought out for their psychic skills and hoodoo work. Such work might include working protective charms, influencing the outcome of a court case, and undoing curses. Some people even said the sisters could read a person's mind, or their future, simply by looking at them. The sisters also apparently maintained their youthful appearance throughout their lives, continuing to look like women in their 20s even in old age. They were also considered identical, and no one knew if they really were seven women, or one woman playing the role of seven sisters.

Another version of the story suggests that there were indeed seven sisters, but the only one who did psychic work was the youngest—the seventh daughter of the family. This would fit with folklore around the world that sees the seventh son or daughter of a family as having psychic gifts, able to issue prophecies or cast curses on people.

The Seven Sisters prove difficult to pin down since different groups lay claim to the name. Author Cathy Smith has written about the folklore around the Seven Sisters of Algiers, named after a New Orleans neighborhood, who worked hoodoo in the area; while others think the Seven Sisters were the daughters of the famous Voodoo Queen, Marie Laveau. According to Voodoo priestess Lilith Dorsey, hoodoo emerged from the conditions of slavery as a way to provide justice for practitioners and its secrets. A set of spiritual practices, traditions, and beliefs, hoodoo was necessary for survival and passed on orally within families. The common misconceptions of both hoodoo and Voodoo have perhaps helped to perpetuate the folklore around the Seven Sisters, creating an air of mystique born from misunderstandings about the African diaspora in North America. It's likely no one will ever know who the sisters truly were—though I'm sure that's exactly how they would want it.

Raven

It's a baking hot day, and a haze hangs low above the tarmac. A black shape flutters above you before landing near a hole in the ground at the edge of the car park. The raven peers into the hole, spotting the water at the bottom that it just can't quite reach. It hops away, returning moments later with a pebble, which it drops into the hole. The bird repeats the action several times until the water level rises and the raven can take a refreshing drink.

Raven Tales are traditional stories from the Indigenous people of the Pacific Northwest coast. They also appear among other First Nation cultures, such as the Inuit of Alaska, Greenland, and northern Canada. Raven is a trickster, one of folklore's ineffable characters who can cause mischief and mayhem, or save the day by using wits rather than brute strength. A creative problem solver, he's able to take on different forms depending on his aims. But unlike other tricksters like Anansi (see page 150), who could sometimes be benevolent, Raven often works to please himself and helping others is an accidental by-product of his actions.

Indigenous groups are not a monolith, and stories and beliefs vary across tribes and regions, although stories may have similarities when explaining the same ideas or concepts—something we see with the Raven Tales. These types of myth help to explain features of the natural world, or they tell the origin stories of groups to preserve their history. Stories also act as cautionary tales to help warn against danger. It's important to respect the fact that certain Indigenous tales are the cultural property of the group or storyteller that created them, and shouldn't be shared without that group's permission. The Raven Tales fall into this category, so the individual tales here have been shared previously, chosen to respect the integrity of Indigenous storytelling.

One legend from the Salish people, retold by the National Library of Medicine as part of their 'Native Voices: Native Peoples' Concepts of Health and Illness' exhibition, explains how Raven's trickery was accidentally beneficial to humanity. A shaman hoarded the world's main light sources: the sun, moon, fire, and stars, hiding them under the sea so that humans could never find them. Raven decided to help, so he disguised himself as a white owl and set out to befriend the shaman. Eventually, Raven won the shaman's trust and when the shaman lowered his guard,

Raven seized his opportunity to steal the hidden lights. Raven let them go one at a time, but he carried the sun the longest. It shriveled his claws and the intense heat turned his feathers black, which explains why the raven has such dark, glossy feathers. In this version of the tale, Raven sets out to help humans, but at a personal cost to himself.

We can't always rely on Raven to help because these tales don't support the good/bad binary familiar in the West.

Another version of this story, told by Haida artist Bill Reid, also thanks Raven for the existence of light in the world. In the time before there was light, the universe was entirely dark because of one old man. He lived by the river and kept the universe's light in the smallest of a series of boxes that nestled inside one another. As the story goes, the old man didn't want to see if his daughter was ugly or beautiful, so he hid the light and they both lived in blissful ignorance. Raven hatched a plan and transformed himself into a hemlock needle to hide in the daughter's drinking water. She swallowed him and became pregnant, eventually giving birth to him as her Raven child. The patriarchal old man accepted his grandson and Raven capitalized on his doting behavior to beg him to open all the boxes. The old man opened them all to keep this Raven child happy, and when he reluctantly opened the smallest box, Raven snatched the light and flew out of the window, taking light into the world. In this version of the story, the superficial old man gets a happy ending too, when it turns out his daughter is beautiful after all (though of course, how good-looking she is shouldn't matter at all when daylight is at stake).

Christian White, a Haida artist, points out that Raven's role as a trickster meant he often brought great change to the world, both by accident and on purpose. In other stories, he also creates the land, discovers humans, and brings fire to the world, making him a force of transformation wherever he goes. Raven acts purely to improve the world for his own benefit, and since we also benefit as a result we can be thankful for his actions, but we can't always rely on him to help because these tales don't support the good/bad binary familiar in the West, and Raven is far more nuanced. Rather than expecting Raven's help, we can instead follow his lesson that creative thinking and challenging authority, especially when that authority harms us, can get us where we need to go.

Raven's status as a trickster depends on his intelligence, and science actually supports this understanding of ravens as birds. Recent studies have shown that ravens are as intelligent as great apes before they even reach maturity, and research also shows that they can even plan and strategize—much like humans. Ravens even build their own tools to help them reach and carry food, and scientists suggest ravens enjoy using them. Ravens can even remember humans who treat them badly and are more friendly towards those that have been nice to them. They're wonderful, clever birds, and the Raven Tales show us how cunning and intentional they truly are. While later versions have been watered down to make Raven less selfish or more caring towards humans, we can learn much about human impulses from the original Raven Tales, and the need to look beyond simplistic binary thinking.

Jack

You're at a storytelling event at your favorite coffeehouse, and the storyteller has the entire audience spellbound as she weaves a tall tale about a kind young man. It seems this young man saw fit to share his food with a poor man, who was no mere poor man—but a magician in disguise! He repays the young man with three wishes, and the young man uses them to protect himself from his abusive stepmother—he's particularly fond of the gift that forces her to loudly break wind whenever she looks at him in an angry or unkind way. It seems the audience enjoy this tale about the young man, Jack, and how could they not? He's been with them in some shape or form since childhood.

The original Jack tales first appeared in print in the 15th century in Britain, as part of a much older oral storytelling tradition. King Arthur himself is considered to be an early prototype for Jack, while tales of Thor's adventures from Snorri Sturluson's *Prose Edda* provide another template for Jack's activities. You've likely already encountered the most famous Jack Tale of all—Jack the Giant Killer, which also appears as Jack and the Beanstalk. Wit, cunning, and cleverness often carry Jack further in his adventures than brute strength alone. While the version of Jack often depicted in pantomime versions of Jack and the Beanstalk seems idealistic, wasting his money on 'magic beans', his actions do also suggest his ability to see beyond obvious solutions, to keep an open mind, and to reap rewards for unconventional behavior.

Scholar Christine L Pavesic suggests that people from Scotland, England, and Ireland took the stories to America in the 18th century, and they appear in print in the 19th century. The stories became especially popular in the Appalachian region of the United States, stretching from New York state in the north and down to Alabama and Georgia in the south. Here, the tales are still part of an active storytelling tradition, having been brought to wider public attention in 1943 when folklorist Richard Chase published a collection of Jack tales. Many of the stories reuse scenarios and characters from the earlier European tales, while reflecting the differences of the Appalachian culture, such as the recognition of Jack's respect for his opponent and his awareness that his opponent underestimates his abilities, giving him an advantage. Jack is sometimes a downtrodden figure who pays someone a kindness, and they give him a magical object that helps him to defeat the story's villain, who

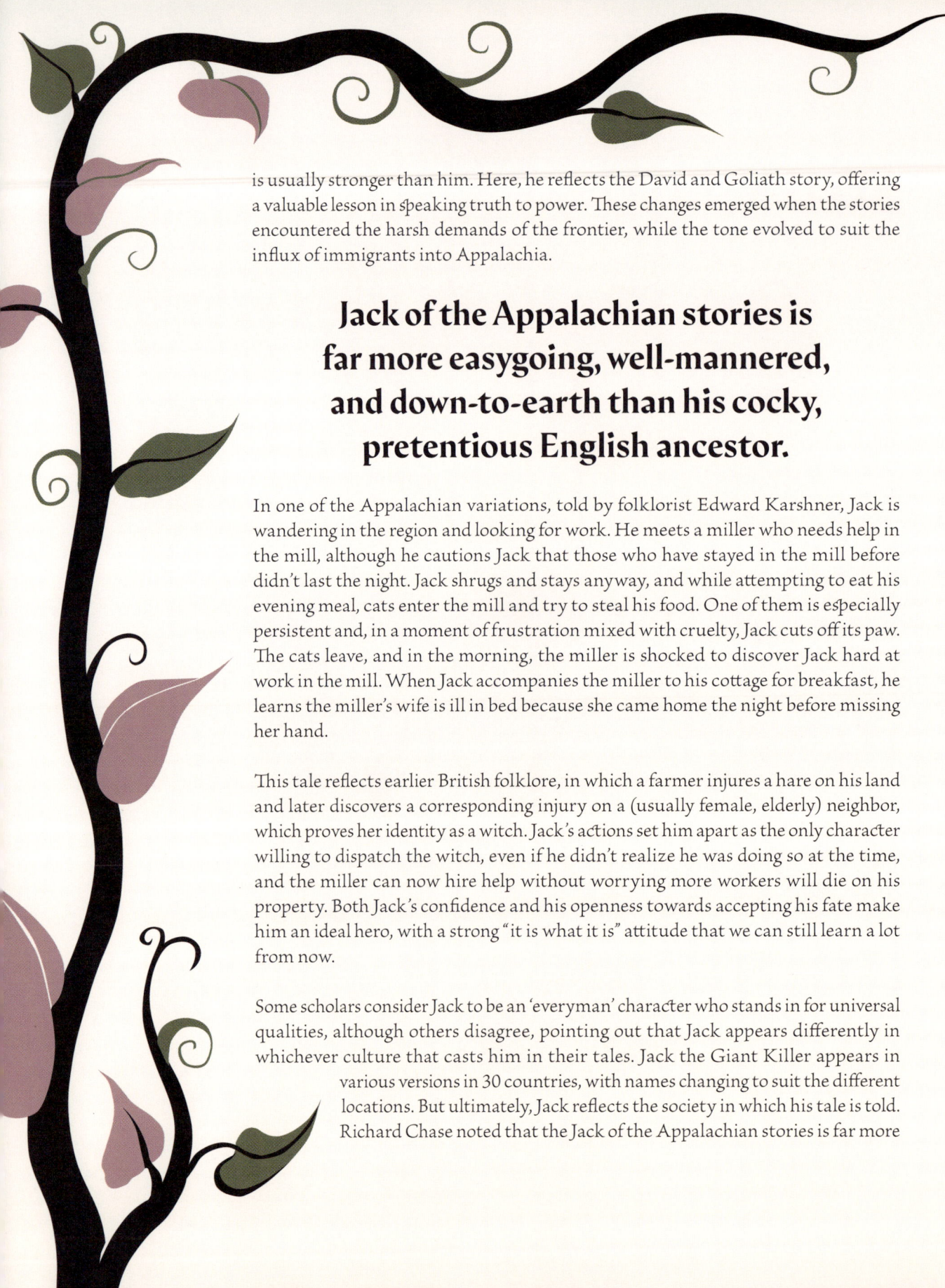

is usually stronger than him. Here, he reflects the David and Goliath story, offering a valuable lesson in speaking truth to power. These changes emerged when the stories encountered the harsh demands of the frontier, while the tone evolved to suit the influx of immigrants into Appalachia.

Jack of the Appalachian stories is far more easygoing, well-mannered, and down-to-earth than his cocky, pretentious English ancestor.

In one of the Appalachian variations, told by folklorist Edward Karshner, Jack is wandering in the region and looking for work. He meets a miller who needs help in the mill, although he cautions Jack that those who have stayed in the mill before didn't last the night. Jack shrugs and stays anyway, and while attempting to eat his evening meal, cats enter the mill and try to steal his food. One of them is especially persistent and, in a moment of frustration mixed with cruelty, Jack cuts off its paw. The cats leave, and in the morning, the miller is shocked to discover Jack hard at work in the mill. When Jack accompanies the miller to his cottage for breakfast, he learns the miller's wife is ill in bed because she came home the night before missing her hand.

This tale reflects earlier British folklore, in which a farmer injures a hare on his land and later discovers a corresponding injury on a (usually female, elderly) neighbor, which proves her identity as a witch. Jack's actions set him apart as the only character willing to dispatch the witch, even if he didn't realize he was doing so at the time, and the miller can now hire help without worrying more workers will die on his property. Both Jack's confidence and his openness towards accepting his fate make him an ideal hero, with a strong "it is what it is" attitude that we can still learn a lot from now.

Some scholars consider Jack to be an 'everyman' character who stands in for universal qualities, although others disagree, pointing out that Jack appears differently in whichever culture that casts him in their tales. Jack the Giant Killer appears in various versions in 30 countries, with names changing to suit the different locations. But ultimately, Jack reflects the society in which his tale is told. Richard Chase noted that the Jack of the Appalachian stories is far more easygoing, well-mannered, and down-to-earth than his cocky, pretentious English ancestor. Here, the Jack stories reflect the ideal qualities of the rural American hinterland, which are far more useful in that context than the English Jack's antics would be.

In some ways, the stories take on a personal dimension as people fold them into their family narratives, where Jack is replaced with aunts, uncles, or distant cousins. People may even swear that the story is absolutely true, even though similar versions appear in so many other families. The nature of Jack remains in these stories, though his qualities of wit, problem-solving, and often kindness are applied to whichever family member takes his place.

Perhaps this is Jack's true role within human society—his adaptability means anyone can have a Jack tale in their ancestry, or even star in one themselves. Jack's positive qualities become aspirational, and they're flexible enough to apply to a range of people in different settings. His enduring popularity is also a testament to the human need to tell and consume stories, since we connect with one another through tales and anecdotes. Jack teaches us the value of common ground between people, where we can communicate at a human level and appreciate our similarities rather than seeking only differences.

Cihuateteo

A terrifying figure kneels at the crossroads, her teeth bared in a menacing snarl, and her fingers bent into vicious claws across her naked chest. Her eyes bulge from her face, which would have once been beautiful but is now stripped of flesh. The Cihuateteo bends over the sacrifice left for her, and you back away.

The Aztecs held childbirth in the same esteem as warfare. Following a baby's safe arrival, the midwife would unleash war cries to show the mother was now a warrior. They also honored those mothers who died in childbirth, considering them as brave warriors for their sacrifice. These lost mothers became the Cihuateteo, or 'divine women'. Such was the level of respect given to these mothers that men would try to steal body parts, such as fingers, of those who died in childbirth to wear in battle for extra courage.

In Aztec mythology, souls went to different realms after death. The Cihuateteo went to Cihuatlampa, the land of women, believed to be in the western sky. By comparison, warriors who fell in battle moved to their own realm of the dead eastern sky. Other realms existed for those who died a watery death, or for dead children, among others. The fallen warriors in the east helped the sun to rise, while the Cihuateteo in the west helped it to set. Yet the Cihuateteo were ambiguous figures, feared and respected in equal measure, believed to seek compensation for their lost lives. The Cihuateteo came to earth for five specific days every year to steal children: they never had the chance to raise their own, so they would take substitutes. Anyone who met them during their time on earth might suffer madness or paralysis.

There is evidence of shrines erected at crossroads—the places where the Cihuateteo were supposed to appear. Crossroads have long been considered a liminal place, or a place between the worlds, because they marked a meeting of roads. It's believed that sacrifices were offered at such shrines, though experts aren't sure if the sacrifices were to please or ward off the spirits.

While the Cihuateteo were death deities, and honored as divine figures, they also represented the precarious nature of childhood and the many dangers it posed to children. These divine women provided a way to make sense of death, and keeping children indoors during their five days on earth could help families to feel safer.

La Llorona

A woman walks alongside the river, peering into the dark water as it bubbles and churns below. Long black hair hangs around her shoulders, and her white dress seems to glow in the moonlight. She looks up at you, stunning you with her beauty, until she opens her mouth and unleashes a mournful wail that strikes terror into the marrow of your bones. La Llorona weeps uncontrollably and she roams off into the darkness, swallowed up by the night.

In one version of the story, La Llorona (or the 'weeping woman') is the most beautiful woman in the village, far out of the league of any of her neighbors. One day, a handsome outsider arrives in the village. She marries him and they have two children, living happily for a while until his eye wanders and he begins courting other women. Driven to despair, La Llorona searches for a way to punish him and, in a fit of spite, drowns their children. The river sweeps away their bodies, and it suddenly dawns on La Llorona what she's done. Hoping to take back her terrible act, she throws herself into the river to look for the children and drowns. She's doomed to search the area forever, weeping as she roams along the river and throughout the hills.

The lover's exploitation of La Llorona provides a parallel with colonialism and its practice of exploiting Indigenous people.

Local parents often use La Llorona as a boogeyman to scare their children into staying close to home. If they stray too far, they risk being picked up by her, who may mistake them for her own children. Some versions of the legend see her carrying a sack as she wanders up and down the river, seeking to spirit away unattended youngsters. The story is most common in Mexico, but it has also spread across North America to the United States, Guatemala, and Costa Rica.

In other versions of the story, La Llorona is from a lower class than her aristocratic lover, and is sometimes Indigenous while he is from Europe. They don't marry, with her upper-class lover exploiting their relationship. She kills the children to prevent her lover from taking them away to be raised by his upper-class new wife.

To some people, the cruel lover's actions cause the tragedy, since he ditches her in favor of a wife of better social standing. Others see La Llorona as a neglectful mother, too absorbed in her lover to treat her children well. The story explores several class distinctions: the difficulties of raising children alone, dysfunctional family dynamics, and the power imbalance between the Indigenous La Llorona and her European lover. The lover's exploitation of La Llorona and threat to remove the children also provides a parallel with colonialism and its practice of exploiting Indigenous people and stealing valuable resources.

In recent years, feminist writers have reinterpreted the legend as an example of women's folklore: tales that preserve and explore issues experienced by those who identify as women. Here, the interpretation sets the infanticide alongside the cruel treatment of La Llorona, with all its racial, class, and gender implications. La Llorona is a complicated figure, since she is both a murderer and a victim. Her story echos that of Medea, a Greek myth in which a callously spurned woman murders her children in grief, and is similarly vilified.

Portrayed as monstrous and violent, La Llorona appears to contradict every stereotype we're told about the inherent nurturing power of mothers. While we can't consider her refusal of this identity as empowering, we can examine the circumstances that created her. Her death and exile from the afterlife are the punishment for her crime, and where she might provide a cautionary tale for wandering children, she also cautions adults to examine the consequences of their own actions. There is another variation of the story in which men spot her wandering in the night and, captivated by her beauty, follow her into the darkness, though they don't get the night of passion they anticipate.

While some scholars think La Llorona steals children because she cannot find her own, others think she is punishing other families since hers broke up. Yet she doesn't attack women or mothers—only children or men. Folklorist Michael Kearney suggests she picks men because they're away from their homes at night, implying they're neglecting their families. He also points out that, unlike many European folktales where human characters can redeem themselves or atone for their sins, La Llorona's punishment is eternal. No amount of anguish for her actions will help her free herself from this torment. In some ways, this recalls the classic ghost stories in which an evil soul is condemned to spend eternity performing a thankless task, like counting blades of grass or spinning ropes out of sand. They can never complete the task, so they're doomed to repeat it. La Llorona can never find her children again, so she's doomed to wander the earth looking for them.

Portrayed as monstrous and violent, La Llorona appears to contradict every stereotype we're told about the inherent nurturing power of mothers.

While many of the elements of the legend may remain the same, the interpretation changes to suit the context in which it is told. Folklorist Ed Walraven, collecting reported 'sightings' of La Llorona, noted that the locations of these sightings are culturally revealing. In North American cities in the 1980s, two sightings were at landfill sites rather than rivers, since infants were more often abandoned in dumpsters than they were drowned.

This shows the archetypal nature of the La Llorona myth, in which aspects of the story (like the setting) can change without affecting the central narrative. It lets people project their own stories or values onto the legend, resurrecting La Llorona as a mournful figure marking her penance for her crime, or casting her as a victim in a situation marked by systemic issues. Choose your La Llorona wisely.

Tlazolteotl

A tall figure stands in the fields, lightning tearing open the dark sky behind her. She wears a headdress decorated with cotton plants, and she suddenly squats, as if about to give birth. The goddess plunges her hands into the rich, dark soil and it almost crackles with new life. The moment passes and Tlazolteotl stands, striding away across the renewed land and into the darkness.

This complex yet fascinating goddess was worshipped as part of the Huaxtec culture in the 10th to mid-15th centuries around the Gulf of Mexico. She's sometimes depicted with black smeared around her mouth, suggesting filth or excrement, or she poses with her mouth wide open, waiting to devour—though quite what she will devour depends on the interpretation. She's linked with cotton plants since they grew abundantly in the region where she was most fervently honored.

Tlazolteotl was an earth goddess, particularly associated with the most fertile black soil, though it's important to remember the land is so fertile because of the decaying matter releasing nutrients back into the ground to nurture new life. Tlazolteotl was linked with this regenerative cycle, the goddess who could take 'rubbish' and turn it into new life. She was also the mother of the maize god and a goddess of fertility, further strengthening her link with life cycles. Some statues also depict her in the process of giving birth, and figurines of Tlazolteotl have been found as an offering to the Cihuateteo, since Tlazolteotl was also sometimes considered a midwife goddess.

But her other associations are more famous and some scholars translate her name to mean 'divine excrement' in Nahuatl. Some of the early sources that survived the Spanish conquest suggest she represented sexual behavior. If enjoyed in moderation, such behavior had associations with the fertility of both humans and the earth itself, while overindulgence could have the opposite effect. Tlazolteotl's ambiguity continued since she both inspired desire and could cleanse people if they'd been sexually excessive thanks to her influence.

In cosmology, this concept is called complementary dualism, and it recognizes that while we find opposing forces throughout nature, we find elements of each force within the other so they can achieve balance, rather than conflict. The two sides

The missionaries saw sexuality and female power as 'bad', and Tlazolteotl became a 'bad' goddess, solely devoted to lust, filth, debauchery, and sin.

actually need each other in order to exist, much like we wouldn't know what darkness was without light to give us its opposite. The most popular understanding of this concept is the yin and yang, where each half contains part of the other, but the worldview does appear in cultures all over the world. When Christian missionaries arrived in Central and South America, they saw things in binary terms and this approach to dualism is based on conflict, with one side being 'good' and the other 'bad'. The missionaries saw sexuality and female power as 'bad', and Tlazolteotl became a 'bad' goddess, solely devoted to lust, filth, debauchery, and sin. To them, sex made you impure and pushed you further away from the divine—there wasn't space in their worldview for the nuanced idea that Tlazolteotl was both divine and sexual.

One 16th-century volume links Tlazolteotl and Eve, describing a festival which involved sweeping roads and houses to drive away evil by keeping them clean. The missionary who wrote the text insisted that the purification feast was intended to remember Eve's sin of eating the fruit from the Tree of Knowledge. They misinterpreted the festival, claiming that people swept the streets to sweep away Tlazolteotl's original sin. Tlazolteotl was also associated with Venus, the Roman goddess of love, lust, and beauty, in an attempt to further link her with humanity's supposedly base instincts.

Tlazolteotl also took four different forms to recognize the life stages of a human. Her first form was as a young woman, carefree and able to tempt people through sexual desire. She became a goddess of gambling in her second form, and her third form was that of a middle-aged yet mighty woman who removed sin. Her fourth form was an old hag who preyed on young people. Her second and fourth forms were the most destructive, associated with the perils of gambling and feeding on young people. This consumption of youth by an aged figure reveals visceral fears about the ageing process. Some writers have linked these four aspects to the moon's four phases, covering the new, waxing, full, and waning moon. This reinforces her role as a goddess associated with cycles, where nothing really ends, instead simply turning into something else.

Studying religion and belief in Central and South America before the 16th-century Spanish Conquest is difficult as Christian missionaries destroyed much of the Indigenous material explaining cultural practices and their deities. They replaced these with their own volumes on the same topics to educate newcomers to the territories, which were full of Christian bias. This makes it difficult to know what among the records is a truly Indigenous interpretation, and what is a Christian misinterpretation of multi-faceted deities and beliefs. Still, the differences between the nuanced Tlazolteotl before the conquest, able to inspire sexual desire and cleanse any sins caused by it, and the negative portrayals after the conquest tell us a lot about the Christian lens used to view her. This binary approach strips her of her original functions, and it also reduces sex to something bad or shameful rather than a natural part of our life cycle. By looking at her again from a complementary dualist perspective, or returning to the Indigenous perceptions of her, we can appreciate just how complex and valuable Tlazolteotl was. She was a goddess associated with agriculture, medicine, cotton, sex, and fertility—not just lust.

Papa Bois

The trees part and a small figure bounds between them, faster than a deer. His cloven hooves make no sound on the forest floor and he blows a blast on a horn. Animals disappear into the depths of the forest, and within moments, you are completely alone. Hunters crash into the clearing, but they won't find anything now that Papa Bois has sounded his warning.

His name means 'Father Wood' or 'Father of the Forest' and he's found in the folklore of St Lucia, Grenada, and Trinidad and Tobago. He also goes by the names Maître Bois ('Master of the Woods') and Daddy Bouchon ('Hairy Man'). According to historian Gerard Besson, stories of Papa Bois date back before the arrival of Europeans in the 15th century, making him one of the oldest figures in Caribbean folklore.

He's usually depicted as a short, muscular old man with cloven hooves, though sometimes he's half-man, half-goat. Hair covers his body, he has a beard made of leaves, and small horns stand proudly on his forehead. Papa Bois protects the forest and its inhabitants, using his bull's horn to warn animals if hunters are approaching. In some legends, he turns into a deer to lure hunters into the forest, where he gets them lost. In other stories, he also treats sick animals in the forest and keeps watch when anyone enters the woods. Some legends claim he turns hunters into wild hogs, doomed to roam in the forest as the target of other hunters.

Papa Bois is the husband or lover of Mama Dlo, or Mama D'Leau, a beautiful woman from the waist up and a snake from the waist down. Her name means 'Mother of the River', and she cares for the river animals. She sometimes punishes those who venture into the forest with destruction in mind, forcing them to become her lover.

As long as you don't mean any harm to the forest, Papa Bois is a positive figure. Though if you encounter him, you must greet him politely and take care not to stare at his hooves. Besson refers to Papa Bois as the only "good" character in the folklore of Trinidad and Tobago, which is otherwise populated with roaming ghosts known as duppies, the jacakalantan light that lures people into danger, La Diablesse (page 94), or the malevolent spirits known as jumbies. But Papa Bois is only good to those who treat the forest with respect. He punishes those who strip the forest for selfish needs, reminding us of the need to be mindful of our relationships with the natural world.

La Diablesse

A tall, statuesque woman sashays along the road in the moonlight. She walks on the grass verge, her large skirts billowing around her. Every now and then, you catch a flash of her muscular thigh as the split in her skirt falls open. The brim of her large hat casts her face into shadow, but you can see eyes burning in the darkness. You don't need to look for her single cloven hoof to know that this is La Diablesse, and you turn your jacket inside out before walking backwards in the direction from which you came.

Named La Diablesse or Ladjablès, her name translates as 'She Devil' or 'Devil Woman' and she's a famous figure in the folklore of Trinidad and Tobago and Grenada. According to the legend, La Diablesse was once human, but she sold her soul to the devil in exchange for eternal youth and beauty, and in return she was turned into a shapeshifting demon.

A tall, striking woman, she wears a long dress with a thigh-high split to show off her supermodel legs. If you do see her, she'll probably be walking along the side of a road. She keeps her human leg visible, and the other in the grass to hide the sound of her cow's hoof foot. Though she has a remarkable figure, her face beneath the veil is described as both corpse-like and hideous. In some stories, her scent is a mixture of decay and expensive perfume.

La Diablesse targets men, luring them into the forest to kill them. In some stories, she meets these men at dances, choosing her target and enchanting him, so he willingly follows her into the darkness in the hope of a saucy encounter. In other stories, she drives men mad and they die by falling into rivers or ravines. Sometimes, she lures them so far into the woods that they become lost, never to be seen again, or are eaten by wild dogs. She apparently poses no danger to women or children.

In some stories, she favors lonely roads and only appears during the full moon. In other legends, she only appears during the day, unlike most nocturnal supernatural creatures. Seeing her does not spell instant doom, though; if you are unfortunate enough to stumble across her, you can turn your clothes inside out and walk away backwards. This breaks her enchantment over you (the method also appears in European folklore as the best way to break fairy spells). Lighting a match or firing up a lighter is also believed to make La Diablesse disappear.

Storyteller Lynn Joseph includes a variation of the legend in *The Mermaid's Twin Sister: More Stories from Trinidad*, which provides an origin for La Diablesse. In this story, a Taíno girl named Suki fell in love with a French captain who landed in Trinidad. They went running together and built a special bond until, sadly, the captain died suddenly. Suki cut off her right foot and left it in his grave so they could continue to run together in spirit, but the newcomers to the island misunderstood her actions. They assumed she killed the captain and drove her into the forest. Thereafter, whenever a man disappeared or died in the woods, they blamed her.

As a furious protector of the women abused by colonialists and plantation owners, La Diablesse is only a figure of fear for those who mean to do harm.

La Diablesse also takes her place in Molinere Underwater Sculpture Park in Grenada's Molinere Bay. British sculptor Jason deCaires Taylor created body casts of local people and turned them into figures from the island's folklore. Placed on the seabed, they provide places for new coral reefs to establish themselves. The La Diablesse figure wears a straw hat, with weeds forming her voluminous skirt, and has an overwhelming power of presence in these ancient waters.

Some say the La Diablesse story is over 300 years old and came from the island of Martinique. French settlers brought her stories to Trinidad where they became common around the villages of the island. These stories describe her dress as being traditional for the island of Martinique, and she hides her hoof in her skirts, rather than the roadside grass. Nineteenth-century writer Lafcadio Hearn included her story in his 1890 book, *Two Years in the French West Indies*, which brought her to wider attention. Storyteller Wendy Shearer notes that she emerges from colonialism, representing the fantasies of the colonists that cast women as exotic. Yet La Diablesse doesn't succumb to any of these fantasies. Instead, she turns them back on the men who would fetishize her for her beauty, leading them to their ultimate doom. Her independence becomes her strength, and she comes to represent freedom from oppression.

This view of La Diablesse as an empowerment icon is a new one, based on the abuse meted out to women in the Caribbean in the past by invading colonial powers. In this contemporary revision, La Diablesse becomes a powerful avenger, destroying those men who are easily tempted away from their lives. As a furious protector of the women abused by colonialists and plantation owners, La Diablesse is only a figure of fear for those who mean to do harm to others, explaining why women and children never find themselves the target of La Diablesse's destructive attention. That she lures men into the forest—where they find themselves vulnerable—also speaks to her role in protecting the island itself, where the features of the land spell doom for enchanted men.

CHAPTER 3

ASIA & OCEANIA

Scheherazade

A young woman sits on a cushion, her face and hands animated as she plunges on through the twists and turns of the tale she tells. A man dressed in rich finery sits beside her, so wrapped up in her words that he can see the picture she paints before him. You notice a younger woman by the storyteller's knee, gazing up at her with fascination. The night passes unnoticed outside as the story unfurls from the storyteller's lips. Before long, you realize you've been woven into Scheherazade's wonderful web of words.

Scheherazade is a major character in *One Thousand and One Nights*, a collection of folktales from southwest Asia that dates to the 12th century, a period described as the Islamic Golden Age. The stories are both entertaining and instructive, often containing valuable lessons for the listener, as oral storytellers passed them down through the generations as a form of social education. 'Sinbad the Sailor' and 'Ali Baba and the 40 Thieves' are among the famous tales, while elements of other stories, including magic lamps and flying carpets, have also become recognizable icons. *One Thousand and One Nights* has influenced writers, filmmakers, composers, artists, and poets around the world.

Scheherazade acts as the storyteller in the overarching narrative that holds the stories together. In the framing story, Shahryar, the sultan, found out his wife had cheated on him, and decided to get his revenge against all women. He would marry a virgin every day, and execute her the following day so she didn't have the chance to betray him. Noble families fled the empire, taking their daughters with them to escape the sultan's bloodthirsty plan. After three years, his vizier ran out of virgins, and to the vizier's horror, his own daughter Scheherazade offered to marry the king. Nothing the vizier said could dissuade her from her plan.

On her wedding night, Scheherazade asked if she could say goodbye to her younger sister. When her sister joined them, she asked Scheherazade for a story. Shahryar agreed, and he listened, spellbound, as Scheherazade told her sister a tale. Dawn broke and Scheherazade stopped in the middle, apologizing to the sultan for speaking so long. Determined to know how the story ended, Shahryar spared her life for another day. Scheherazade finished the story that night, but

also began another, which she also stopped in the middle. This went on, with Shahryar sparing her life each night until she'd told 1,000 stories. By this point, Scheherazade had run out of stories, but Shahryar had fallen in love with her and he spared her as his queen.

Scheherazade has rightfully become a popular character since she wins the sultan over with her intelligence, storytelling abilities, and charm. She is also a hero because her storytelling postpones any further marriages, stopping any more executions for the duration of her speaking (and beyond, since the sultan falls for her). Her bravery in putting herself directly in harm's way is also a testament to her confidence that her plan will work. It's not up to her to escape from tyranny, but rather to work from the inside to change the tyrant's mind. She acts to resolve a situation that everyone else has accepted as simply how things must be, knowing that things can be different.

In using her stories as lessons for the sultan, Scheherazade's stories also become lessons for readers, giving her power to change hearts and minds through her tales.

This framing story also runs counter to the trend in Western fairy tales for couples to meet, fall in love, and marry within days, barely giving themselves time to get to know each other. Scheherazade and the sultan instead enjoy a relationship rooted in creativity, while the sultan's regard for Scheherazade grows from his enjoyment of her talents, rather than simply her looks. Where figures like Snow White score romantic victories through being "the fairest of them all," Scheherazade is a much more rounded character, offering greater potential for female achievement, solidarity, and liberation.

Some scholars have noted the apparent misogyny within the stories themselves, though it's also important to remember they reflected the times that produced them. Keeping the context in mind helps us to view the stories as a portrait of the original culture, adding historical value to the tales. Many of the stories that feature women as adulteresses appear at the start of the collection, when Scheherazade first tells her tales. By reflecting the sultan's view back to him, she can win him over more easily because these duplicitous women confirm what he already believes. She introduces more nuance in the later stories once she earns his trust, until she can include intelligent and compassionate women that he accepts since he has come to accept these qualities in her. The later stories include women as rulers, warriors, scholars, and entrepreneurs, and their remarkable behavior works to shift the sultan's opinion of women altogether. This approach makes Scheherazade even more impressive, showing us her grasp both of psychology and human nature, but also her ability to see the sultan's potential for change.

In recent years, Scheherazade has become a role model for Muslim women, offering inspiration as a visionary changemaker who works within her culture, not against it. The story also shows the power of education, since it is Scheherazade's study of a vast range of topics that provides her with the tools to tell her stories. Bouthaina Shaaban, professor of English literature at Damascus University, points out Scheherazade's power in diffusing a culture of violence using language and imagination—something that should be an inspiration to us even now. In using her stories as lessons for the sultan, Scheherazade's stories also become lessons for readers, giving her the power to change hearts and minds through her tales right across the centuries since they were written. It's an excellent reminder of the ability of art to speak truth to power, but also to change a person's perspective, since art needs emotional involvement from its audience. Scheherazade is an important leader in this, and she shows us the difference one person can make with the right words.

Jinn

You're sitting on the sofa of a friend's house, chatting about this and that. Nothing seems amiss, until a little voice pipes up on the other side of the room. It's your toddler cousin, and she's engaged in an enthusiastic conversation... only you can't see who she's talking to. She keeps pausing, letting her unseen companion reply to her babble. Prickles creep across your skin, especially since the cat stands in the doorway, back arched and eyes wide, teeth bared in a hiss. Only a jinn could explain this strange domestic scene before you.

Jinn, also referred to as djinn, appear in the Quran as one of Allah's creations, alongside humans and angels. A research study in 2012 by Pew Research Center found that more than half of Muslims surveyed believed in jinn, though the exact totals varied by region. Jinn predate the Quran, though it's difficult to know exactly where they came from since they appear in ancient myths and folklore from southwest Asia. Scholar Amira El-Zein notes the importance of jinn within Islam, and understanding jinn can help people to understand Islam itself. She also points out that their ambiguity, with jinn just one decision away from benevolence or destruction, makes them a complex area of study.

In Islamic scripture, Allah created the first jinni (the singular form of jinn) from a scorching desert wind, and jinn ruled the earth long before the creation of humans. The name actually means 'hidden', and though we can't see them, they're believed to exist all around us. The Quran describes them as being made of smokeless fire, and while they're invisible, they can still interact with the material world. Jinn can fly, shapeshift, move between dimensions, and possess humans, but they can also live their own lives completely separate from mankind. Jinn eat, marry, have children, and die, although they live longer than humans, so, compared to us, they might as well be immortal. Since they have free will, just like humans, they can be good, bad, or neutral, depending on their own choices. They can even reproduce with humans, and some legends paint the Queen of Sheba as being half-jinn, half-human.

It's difficult to describe what jinn look like because they rarely reveal themselves in their true form. Some legends explain this is because humans can't comprehend the actual appearance of the jinn. Instead, they only see jinn when the jinn allow it, and in the form the jinn chooses. They can transform into humans up to a point, but they

can't disguise their backwards-facing feet, which often give them away in encounters. They're most likely to adopt the form of the snake, and the only form they can't take is that of the wolf, which are protective figures who hunt jinn. While humans often move through life completely unaware of jinn, animals can apparently sense them, which could explain all those times you find your cat staring in fright at an apparently empty corner.

Over the centuries, humans have used a range of methods to contact and control the jinn, including ritual invocations, or making rings and talismans. Even King Solomon could command the jinn using his ring, and he subsequently appears in different stories, wherein someone finds a vessel in which the king has trapped a jinni. 'The Fisherman and the Jinni' appears in *One Thousand and One Nights*. In this story, a fisherman finds a sealed bottle in the sea. He opens it, unleashing a furious jinni who seeks to end whoever frees him, but through some clever wordplay the fisherman ends up with fine fishing success.

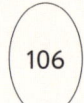

There are beliefs around changelings with jinn and fairies, in which the otherworldly creatures swap a human child for one of their own.

Some jinn are happy to live their lives with no contact with humans, while others enjoy toying with people as entertainment. According to podcaster Rabia Chaudry, there are different categories of jinn, which include neutral jinn who live alongside us inside our homes and protective jinn who love babies and small children, which explains why children often converse with apparently invisible figures. There are also evil jinn, which includes the ifrit—the biggest, fastest, and most evil of the malign jinn. They're the closest to demons; the genie from *One Thousand and One Nights* is actually an ifrit. That might make you rethink the genie in *Aladdin*. Finally, ghouls are also jinn; monstrous figures that hide in cemeteries. Some of them will only venture near humans when they want to feed.

According to Islamic literature, we also all have a qareen, which is a constant life companion from birth to death. The idea of a constant spirit companion echoes the daemons of Philip Pullman's *His Dark Materials* trilogy, but unlike these spirits (the animal embodiment of our inner selves), the qareens are independent beings that

choose us. Some think the qareen is a guardian spirit, while others think they try to persuade us to do what is bad for us. Just as the qareen is free to decide if it wants to entice us towards good or evil, we can choose how we want to act.

Chaudry also notes the similarity of jinn stories with those of European fairies, both of which predate humans and withdrew from living alongside humans. There are beliefs around changelings with jinn and fairies, in which the otherworldly creatures swap a human child for one of their own. These stories may have been a way for people to understand unexplained illness or strange behavior in a child, with horrific 'cures'—such as switching the changeling back for the 'real' child by leaving it in a cemetery. Iron will ward off both jinn and fairies; some types of jinn even sound like dragons and vampires and like fairies, jinn can be both tricksters and inspirational amuses.

Genies have become famous in Western pop culture via *Aladdin, The X Files, Buffy the Vampire Slayer*, and *I Dream of Jeannie,* but jinn are far richer, and far less benevolent, than these sanitized (and often whitewashed) versions would have you believe. Jinn sometimes feature in horror films, and the Iranian film *Under the Shadow* was one of the most successful in exploring the impact of jinn on humans. Ultimately, jinn are perhaps more like humans than we might like to believe, capable of good, evil, and everything in between.

Churel

A figure shuffles along the road, her feet pointing in one direction while she faces the opposite way. Her hands twist into claws and a mane of tangled hair spills down her back. If you saw the churel head-on, you'd see she has tusks and fangs. A man appears and the figure before you transforms, becoming a tall, elegant woman with beautiful hair. Before you can shout a warning, she leads him away down a track to his doom.

The legend of the churel, sometimes called a churail, started in Persia, though now it's most often found in South Asia, particularly in Pakistan, Bangladesh, and India. The churel is a woman who returns after death as a vampire. She's usually pictured as ugly, though she will shapeshift into a beautiful woman to beguile men. The churel wanders in lonely places, using her hypnotic gaze to lead her victim somewhere quiet where she drinks their blood. With her feet facing the other direction, she walks backwards while keeping her eyes on you. Sometimes you can tell one is nearby if you hear her shell bangles rattling.

Some versions of the legend claim that if a pregnant woman dies during the Hindu festival of Diwali, she will return as a churel. Others say a woman dying during childbirth creates the churel. A woman might also become a churel if her family mistreats her, a fear which led to families taking good care of female relatives, particularly when they're pregnant. If a family fails to do so, the churel might target them. Other legends say she only kills the men in her family, starting with whoever mistreated her. But if she's buried with the right care and respect, she may not return as a churel. While her victims are usually adults, teenage boys are sometimes at risk from her bloodlust. There is also a way to avoid a grisly fate if you encounter one— block her mesmerizing gaze by putting a cloth over your eyes.

The legend might sound horrific, and it's distressing that a family would need the threat of a monster to treat a pregnant woman well, but the churel does at least ensure they're cared for at a vulnerable time. Some writers have tried to reclaim the churel as a feminist icon since she avenges her mistreatment, targeting aggressive or neglectful men as a way for women to fight back against oppressive behavior. Like La Llorona (see page 84), the churel is created by her circumstances, making her a victim as well as a monster.

Taraka

The monster Taraka stands before you, a terrifying vision that inspires both awe and dread. Tusks curve upwards from the corners of her mouth, a mouth spread wide in a menacing grin. The worst part? You know she has a taste for human flesh.

Taraka, also called Tataka in some sources, is cast as a villain in the *Ramayana*, a Sanskrit epic from 650-350 BCE. The overarching story features a hero, Rama, who faces different challenges in his quest to rescue his wife. One of these challenges includes killing Taraka, a giant, fierce monster who jealously guards her forest and eats anyone who dares venture within its borders. Yet Rama proves curious, and asks how it is that she came to be such a powerful monster. According to legend, she was a nature spirit with the strength of 1,000 elephants. After a sage killed her husband, Taraka swore revenge. The sage cursed her when she attacked him, condemning the grief-stricken nymph to become a monstrous cannibal. Her hideous appearance became an external manifestation of her fury.

At first, Rama hopes to cut off her ears and nose so she can't hear or smell people coming, but she attacks him and he kills her with an arrow.

One reading of this story is as a caution against female power or rage. The heroes that destroy rampaging female figures in such tales are usually male, and their defeat of the female monster restores the patriarchal status quo. But that isn't always how these stories have been received, even centuries ago. Often, these figures are actually viewed as sympathetic in their rage against the machine.

The story itself isn't sympathetic to Taraka, but the poem doesn't condemn her purely for being female, as we can sometimes see in other legends in which a female character becomes monstrous (poor Medusa, rendered fearsome as a punishment and then destroyed to suit a whim of the gods, is the best example of this). Instead, the poem shows Taraka as monstrous because of her preference for strength and violence, rather than accepting what has happened and grieving her loss. The sage notes that even women should face punishment if they perpetrate evil acts—the actions are the focus, not the gender. The fact her son is likewise cursed to become a demon shows the punishment fits the crime, rather than the gender expression of the figure, since preserving peace is Rama's paramount aim.

Jeoseung Saja

The doors to the hospital ward swing open and a tall man in a long black coat and a black hat walks in. The nurses don't look up, seemingly unaware that he's here. He drifts along the ward, ignoring the beds on either side of him, until he reaches the one nearest the window. An old man lies sleeping, the overhead lights reflecting yellow on his waxy skin. The Jeoseung Saja bends over the bed, and the old man wakes up. He starts when he sees the pale figure, but nods once. The man in black helps him out of bed and leads him out of the corridor. The patient's heart machine flat lines once the ward doors swing closed behind him.

The Jeoseung Saja is a Korean depiction of Death that is very different from the typical 'skeleton in a robe with a scythe' that we see in Western popular culture. 'Jeoseung' translates as 'afterlife', while 'Saja' means 'messenger', so these beings are more like couriers than Grim Reapers. It's their job to fetch and escort the newly dead along Hwangcheon Road, the road that leads to the afterlife. Some writers explain they are spirits working for King Yeomna, who rules the underworld and judges the souls of the dead.

The myths about these beings date back to the Joseon era, which began in 1392 and ended in 1910, and the earliest incarnations wore fine black clothing and the same wide black hat worn by civil servants. Over time, artists and filmmakers have explored updated costumes to suit new eras, but each version always wears a black hat. In some versions of their legend, they carry red cloths that bear lists of the names of those who will die. They read each name three times—then, the person has to follow them out of the world of the living. In other legends, the Jeoseung Saja simply appears at the point of death, ready to escort the soul to the afterlife. These latter stories see the figures wandering in places most often associated with death, like hospitals or towns where disease is rife.

Not everyone is willing to go quietly with the Jeoseung Saja when their time comes. One myth tells the story of General Sineui, who wanted to cheat death. He planted a ring of orange trees around his house, since oranges had the power to guard against evil. A Jeoseung Saja arrived, intending to claim Sineui, but he couldn't pass the ring of protective orange trees. The Jeoseung Saja patrolled the grounds beyond the trees for four days, when he suddenly spotted a peach tree. He passed beneath its branches and entered the house, where he met Sineui. The general wore a silver pin, since silver also protected against evil, but the Jeoseung Saja hid until Sineui went to wash, before hitting Sineui with an iron hammer to claim his soul.

While people fear these beings, that the Jeoseung Saja wear the clothing of civil servants brings an air of organization, and even bureaucracy, to the process of death.

As part of his plan to cheat death, Sineui had left instructions to his family that they should wait a week to bury him, allowing enough time for his soul to escape from the underworld. But it took too long for Sineui to return. His family had buried him by the time his soul found his body, so Sineui suffocated in his grave and died a second time. The Jeoseung Saja made sure Sineui stayed in the afterlife this time. This myth demonstrates that you cannot bargain with or bribe a Jeoseung Saja. When it's your time to leave the mortal world, you have no choice but to go with them.

The living sometimes see the Jeoseung Saja after someone dies, so these figures are sad omens of loss and people understandably want to avoid them. Some people believe that seeing one means you will be the next to die and even dreaming of them is a bad omen. It's important to remember that the Jeoseung Saja don't cause people's deaths, they're simply there to collect the soul. While people fear these beings, that the Jeoseung Saja wear the clothing of civil servants brings an air of organization, and even bureaucracy, to the process of death.

Their human appearance makes them feel more comforting at a deeply traumatic time, and they play the role of a "psychopomp," leading the soul to where it needs to go next. Psychopomps (spirits tasked with guiding a person to the afterlife) appear in mythology and belief systems all over the world, and famous examples include the Grecian figure of

Hermes, the Valkyries of Norse myth, and even animals like dogs and crows. Some people also believe their ancestors or departed loved ones will come to get them when they die.

The Jeoseung Saja has enjoyed a resurgence of popularity in recent years thanks to its inclusion in *Guardian: The Lonely and Great God*, a 2016 Korean drama. The drama followed the exploits of an immortal Joseon-period general, and a Jeoseung Saja took the character of the general's best friend. The figure of the Jeoseung Saja continued to appear in further installments of the show, although these later series adapted the Jeoseung Saja's folklore, changing the way in which it interacts with humans. The inclusion of the figure allowed the programme makers to explore topics such as trauma in a more compassionate way, something that is common to fictional narratives that include Death as a personified character.

It's possible to view these figures as an example of death positivity, since they act as companions, albeit briefly, ensuring the scared and confused soul doesn't get lost. Even though they're not human, psychopomps appear at the moment when we're most vulnerable to walk by our side, and this can certainly be a comforting thought. They also remind us that while life and death sound like a binary, it's often more complex than that, with something of a grey area between life and the afterlife. Psychopomps dwell in these liminal grey areas to ease the transition from one state to the next, and we should probably thank them for that.

Okiku

Shadows gather in the corners of the courtyard and silence creeps through the empty corridors. You stare at the well in the yard, and as if on cue, a beautiful young woman with long black hair rises from the depths. She mutters to herself, as though counting something that only she can see. The numbers abruptly stop and she unleashes a bloodcurdling scream that echoes throughout the castle from its lowest dungeon to its highest tower.

If the emergence of a long-haired girl from a well sounds like a familiar image, then you would be right, since many believe the legend of Okiku served as an inspiration for Koji Suzuki's novel *Ringu*, which was adapted as a popular horror film, *Ring*, in both Japan and the US. Before the novel and the films, the kabuki play *Banchō Sarayashiki* had already popularized the story. The legend became one of the 'Nihon san dai kaidan' ('Japan's Three Great Ghost Stories').

Okiku works as a servant, washing dishes at Himeji Castle (although the location changes depending on the tale). She catches the eye of Aoyama, a samurai who works for her master, who tries to seduce her to no avail. The unpleasant Aoyama won't take no for an answer and hides a valuable plate from a set of 10, knowing that losing even one carries the death penalty. Aoyama tries to blackmail Okiku into becoming his mistress, threatening to tell their master she stole the plate. Okiku still won't give in, so she drowns herself in the mansion's well to escape Aoyama's advances. In some even darker variations of the story, Aoyama tortures Okiku to force her into becoming his mistress, and her continual refusals prompt him to murder her.

Yet Okiku gets her revenge from beyond the grave. Her ghost appears every night, wandering the castle and its grounds, counting one to nine to mark the remaining plates. Once she reaches nine, she howls and sobs for hours. Her appearances, and the accompanying screaming, drive the samurai mad. In one legend, anyone who heard any of the counting fell ill, but anyone who heard her reach nine died within days, reflected in *Ringu*'s time-based haunting.

There are variations to the story, though they all include the sobbing ghost in the well. One version shows Okiku breaking the plate by accident, and her enraged master kills her and throws her body into the depths. In another, the samurai's

OKIKU

117

JAPAN

jealous wife breaks the plate and frames Okiku. A third version sees Okiku reveal a plot by her master against the local lord. When her master discovers her role in the drama, he throws her into the well. In another version, Aoyama doesn't just want to seduce Okiku, he wants to marry her. She doesn't love him so she refuses, and in a fit of toxic masculinity, he tries to manipulate her into marrying him anyway. There's even a different ending, in which the lord asks a priest to come and lay Okiku's ghost to rest. He waits by the well at night, and as predicted, the ghost emerges and begins counting. When Okiku reaches nine, the priest shouts "10!" and Okiku vanishes for good, relieved the tenth plate had been found.

The imbalance of power between the samurai and the servant helps to add to the injustice of the tale, since Okiku has no avenues of possible help.

In illustrations of the story, Okiku often wears a white dress, with her long black hair flowing loose, much like the ghost in the *Ringu* films. In Japan, people who die in unnatural circumstances become yūrei, a type of ghost. The name yūrei translates to 'faint soul' or 'dim spirit', and these ghosts are stuck on earth to finish their task before they can move on. In Okiku's case, this keeps her counting the plates until the missing one is 'found' by the priest. With the problem resolved, she is finally free to go. Surprisingly, the lower the person was on the social scale, the more powerful they became as a yūrei, adding an interesting class dynamic to these stories.

Despite the variations, certain elements remain the same. Okiku is always a female servant from a lower class who is killed or driven to suicide by a man of a higher class. Her ghost always returns every night to count and wail, fixated on the nine plates that remain intact. Aoyama always ends up driven insane, with Okiku's howls becoming a manifestation of his guilt for his part in her death. The imbalance of power between the samurai and the servant helps to add to the injustice of the tale, since Okiku has no avenues of possible help. In the variations where she's accused of theft or breaking the plate, she never speaks up for herself, perhaps because she knows no one will believe her— highlighting the sad reality of whose voices are heard and trusted, an issue that continues into the 21st century. The story also undercuts the samurai's honor code with Aoyama's manipulative behavior, helping to further paint him as the legend's villain.

Okiku is sometimes described as an onryō, which is a spirit that seeks vengeance against whoever wrongs them. While her screams punish Aoyama, her frantic counting sounds more like a replay of her terrified actions when she discovers the missing plate. It's important that the priest does not banish or exorcize Okiku, but helps her to let go and be at peace. The priest's kind decision to help her reach the number 10 allows her to release her grasp on the woe of her mortal life. After all, Okiku does nothing wrong in any variation of the story. She always maintains her values and principles, refusing to compromise them even in the face of certain death. The haunting functions to right a wrong and attain the justice denied to Okiku in life.

In 1795, Japan's wells suffered from a larvae infestation, later called the "Okiku insect." People blamed Okiku's ghost for the infestation, as though her sadness manifested as tangible insects. Himeji Castle claims the well in its grounds is the exact well from the story, and even has bars over it. While some claim Okiku wasn't laid to rest and still haunts the area, the various retellings of her legend help to preserve this sad tale of manipulation and justice from beyond the grave.

Nang Tani

The full moon hangs low in the sky, casting its soft, silvery glow across a grove of banana trees. A figure flits between the trees, inspecting the bunches of flowers left beside them. A curtain of black hair ripples across her shoulders; her skin is the same shade of green as the trees.

According to Thai folklore, Nang Tani appears as a young woman wearing a traditional green Thai dress with bare feet in wild banana tree groves. She's usually only seen during a full moon, and is thought to avenge women who have been mistreated by men (though the legends aren't always clear about how she does this). In some stories, Nang Tani even offers food to monks.

Other stories disagree with the vengeance perspective, explaining that single men might choose to marry Nang Tani. According to some writers, men can summon her by urinating on one of her trees. A spirit marriage isn't without complication: Nang Tani would drain their life-force during sex, and they would require her permission to sleep with anyone else afterwards.

She's a popular spirit among Thailand's ghosts. While she's usually considered to be gentle, cutting down her trees will bring bad luck to everyone involved, and so locals refuse to fell them, though the bananas are inedible. Despite her apparent docility, people still try to avoid living near wild banana trees, perhaps being wary of angering her. Locals tie a red cloth around the trees she haunts, marking them as being off-limits. They also leave sweets or flowers as offerings, hoping she will bring them good fortune and protection.

Both the flowers and leaves of the wild banana trees are used in medicinal remedies, though they're believed to have magical properties, too. The value of the leaves and flowers could explain the cautionary aspect of the tale against cutting down the trees. Yet there is another explanation. Animism lies at the heart of Thai lore, a worldview that sees everything from trees to rivers to mountains as having their own spirits. Nang Tani represents the spirit of the banana trees, explaining the importance of not felling them. In this worldview, humans are just one part of an interconnected community alongside their animal, botanical, and mineral neighbors, and must treat the natural world with respect.

Meng Po

It's dark and miserable as you shuffle along, trying to keep your place in the queue. An elderly woman stands beside a bridge up ahead, a bubbling cauldron beside her. You can't identify the smell that wafts towards you, both bitter and sweet at the same time, but it brings a small spark of comfort in a dismal place. The woman ladles soup into the outstretched cups that pass her, and you realize this must be Meng Po. After you drink your soup, you will remember absolutely nothing.

Sometimes known as Granny or Aunt Meng, Meng Po is a goddess of forgetfulness in Diyu, the Chinese underworld. Everyone will pass through Diyu after they die, but the length of time spent there varies depending on what you did while you were alive. Souls might be repeatedly dunked into boiling oil, crushed by heavy carts, or endlessly bitten by snakes. Once you were punished for your sins in the court of hell dedicated to that punishment, you passed to the tenth court, where you were reincarnated. While the torments of Diyu might sound like the Western version of the Christian hell, it's not run by any devils or demons, and the demons in Diyu have no influence over humans while they're alive.

After you drink your soup, you will remember absolutely nothing.

Meng Po has a special job as part of this process, serving the souls of the dead her Meng Po soup, which removes their memories of both Diyu and their life on earth so they can reincarnate without them. Her 'Five Flavored Tea of Forgetfulness' is made of the tears a soul cried when they were alive and a mysterious blend of herbs. The tea's Chinese name translates as the 'waters of oblivion'. Sometimes, things don't go quite to plan and the soul doesn't drink the tea. When this happens, children remember their past lives and there are stories of newborns who can talk.

It's likely Meng Po first appeared in China in the 1st century CE, but some myths describe her origins as even older. In one variation, she was a mortal woman called Lady Meng Jiang. Her husband died after being conscripted to build the Great Wall, and her grief was so all-consuming that Meng Jiang couldn't reincarnate. Determined that no one else should suffer the same way, she invented her tea to induce amnesia.

Another origin story in *The Jade Guidebook*, an 11th-century Daoist text about the underworld, depicts Meng Po as a Buddhist hermit who lost herself in the scriptures and couldn't tell the past and future apart. In this text, she's described as being 81, with white hair, and a childlike complexion.

In some legends, Meng Po greets the dead at the entrance to the ninth court of Diyu, while in others, she lives in the tenth court, or the final court before reincarnation. The number of levels, or courts, in hell varies according to Taoism, Buddhism, and folklore. In *The Jade Guidebook*, Meng Po sits on a throne and she dishes out cups of soup to souls who shuffle past her in the queue. In other, more popular versions of the legend, she waits beside the Naihe Bridge, or Bridge of Helplessness. The bridge is several miles long yet only three fingers wide. Even more perilous, there are no railings so there's nothing to stop you from tumbling into the blood river that flows below. If you were unlucky enough to fall off, you'd never be reincarnated.

Meng Po becomes a comforting presence to many because she makes sure no one remembers their horrific time in hell. To some, this is a small kindness given the awful things that happen to souls in Diyu (though in *The Jade Guidebook*, souls are forced to drink the soup whether they like it or not). To others, it's a great shame because it means you lose any and all knowledge you managed to accrue while you were alive. You don't cease to exist, because your Karma passes along with you, but 'you' as you exist now, with all your memories, ideas, and quirks, will disappear.

The soup's amnesiac effects are irreversible. In some ways, it's reminiscent of Greek mythology, where the dead drank from the River Lethe on their way into the underworld to wash away their memories of their mortal life. But Meng Po's soup is drunk before reincarnation, not eternal life in the underworld. At least, that's the theory. Some have theorized that the wave of instinctual love or hate that we feel when we meet a stranger might be a ghost of a memory not entirely wiped by Meng Po's soup.

The process of reincarnation underlines the cyclical nature of existence, with birth, life, death, and rebirth a reminder that whatever we experience now won't last forever.

Meng Po becomes a reminder of our own mortality, but also our immortality. While everything we learned, knew, and experienced in one life will be obliterated, our soul continues. We can draw some comfort from the idea of forgetting everything in our life, particularly for those of us who have suffered trauma, hardship, and pain. But the process of reincarnation underlines the cyclical nature of existence, with birth, life, death, and rebirth a reminder that whatever we experience now won't last forever.

Huli Jing

It's a few moments after sunset and a flash of silver fur crosses your path, nine sleek tails rippling behind it. You blink, and the creature is gone. Instead, a beautiful woman stands nearby, wrapped in a silvery gown that glitters in the faint moonlight. You're not sure how to greet a huli jing, so you back away before she notices you.

Huli jing, which translates as 'fox spirit', are shape-shifting spirits in Chinese folklore. They're ambiguous figures, either helpful or dangerous depending on the story, but they're most famous for being able to turn into beautiful young women to seduce men. In some stories, the huli jing appeared when foxes learned to use magic.

The most famous of the huli jing is the Jiuwei Hu, the silvery fox spirit with nine tails. The Jiuwei Hu first appeared in the 4th century BCE book, *Classics of Mountains and Seas*, where it was described as a man-eating beast that howled like a baby. If you managed to capture one, eating its meat would protect you from being poisoned. The book claimed the creature lived in Qingqiu, or 'Green Hills', considered a deeply magical location. Despite their man-eating tendencies, seeing a Jiuwei Hu was a good omen since they only made appearances in areas that were quiet and peaceful. You wouldn't want to get too close to the Jiuwei Hu, but seeing one showed you were safe where you were.

People considered the huli jing as perilous because they would drain their partner's life force until the man was energetically empty; the fox spirit would then move onto a new partner. In some tales, they can become immortal if they drain enough energy from humans. Some writers have suggested this was simply bad PR to try and stop men from pursuing relationships with these sultry beings, while others hint that the spirits got so tired of being cast as the villain that they decided to go along with it.

As shapeshifters, the huli jing can wreak havoc depending on the form they choose to take. In some stories, they appear as someone close to their target who died, which either lets them woo their intended victim, or traumatizes them. An angry huli jing can drive humans insane, so appearing as someone that would make a human trust them can avoid this scenario.

Others disagree, saying that huli jing follow Taoist principles, making them both wiser and more just than humans. While their main ambition is becoming immortal and being able to use magic, hurting humans doesn't figure in their game plan. If anything, these stories show how helpful the huli jing can be. In one story from around 239 BCE, the legendary ruler Yu the Great heard about a girl in Tushan who claimed she was a fox spirit. She expressed an interest in starting a family with the ruler, and so Yu the Great married her and they had a son together. The huli jing came to represent both royalty and fertility.

A variation on this legend is that Yu the Great was trying to save his people from a flood, when a Jiuwei Hu appeared. It turned itself into a woman so it could help him, and in true 'happy ever after' fashion, fell in love with him. Yu was famous for his engineering ability to tame the frequent floods that devastated the land—his flood control measures allowed the people to use the mighty rivers for irrigation. Some people think that the woman was actually from a tribe that had a nine-tailed fox as a symbol, but the magical version seems to be more apt.

Any time a woman becomes a little too powerful for the liking of those around her, she gets branded as evil, destructive, lustful, or a 'homewrecker' (all titles also applied to the huli jing).

Up until the Tang Dynasty, of the 7th to the 10th centuries, the Huli jing were shown as benevolent and peaceful. After this point, the spirits gained their bad reputation, more often considered as demons that wanted to steal power from humans. These fox spirits grew another tail every time they obtained more magical power. Folklorist Keith Stevens points out that even the painful practice of foot binding was linked to the huli jing: the Shang empress Daji apparently started the tradition, and people believed she was a fox spirit in disguise, binding her paws so that no one would realize her true nature.

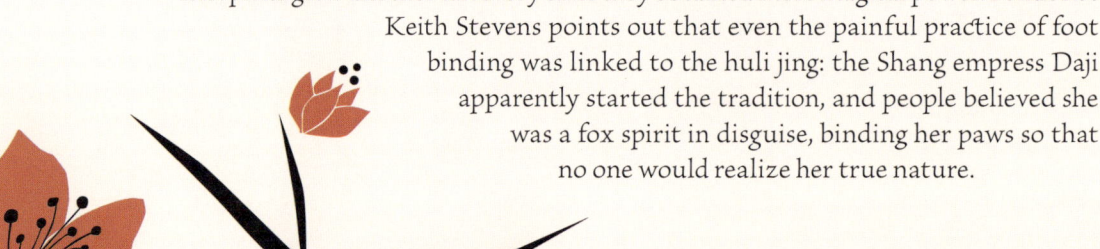

Some writers think the huli jing's change in reputation came about because of two queens who managed to end powerful dynasties. They wrought so much damage that people assumed they had to be magical creatures who manipulated men to get their own way. We see similar moves any time a woman becomes a little too powerful for the liking of those around her; she gets branded as evil, destructive, lustful, or a 'homewrecker' (all titles also applied to the huli jing).

Stevens writes that some people even thought the huli jing made their homes in graves during the day, only venturing out after sunset. This idea certainly helps to draw other parallels with vampires, with the huli jing sucking out energy instead of blood. People did, and still do, revere the huli jing, though they weren't worshipped since they are not deities. Some people left offerings for them, understanding that this would 'buy' their good opinion and might even help to improve their finances or health. Granting them a level of respect recognized the dangers an offended huli jing might pose. Shamans would even test brides to make sure they were humans, and not shapeshifting fox spirits. A shaman might go into a trance and draw blood from his arm, which was made into a charm to protect the human that carried it.

In folklore, the huli jing help and befriend humans, and sometimes fall in love with them. Others trick them to drain the human's essence. In many ways, they're similar to humans: some of us try to be helpful, positive, and kind people, while others are toxic, manipulative, and dangerous. It's unsurprising that people consider the fox spirits to be sly, cunning, clever, and seductive, since these are all characteristics also ascribed to foxes. They're also human traits, so perhaps we have more in common than we think.

Barong

A large creature capers through the trees. Thick white fur covers its back, while its gold jewelry, adorned with small mirrors, jangles as it moves. It turns its red face towards you, staring with protruding eyes, and fangs curving out of its mouth like tusks. A dark beard of human hair hangs below its grin, though you can't help yourself from returning its smile. You sense this mighty creature is Barong, a playful spirit that poses no threat as long as you come in peace.

In Bali, Barong is the king of the spirits, and he represents all that is good. As a symbol of both good fortune and health, Barong is much older than Hinduism, part of an ancient form of animism. He's considered a protective spirit over the Balinese and each region of Bali has its own Barong. Some scholars think the name 'Barong' comes from the word 'bahrwang', which is Sanskrit for 'bear', although Barong now takes the form of different animals. While the Barong Ket is a lion and the most popular form, Barong can also be a boar, an elephant, a snake, a tiger, or a dog.

Some writers consider this spirit a form of guardian angel, and the Banas Pati Raja spirit from every villager combines to animate Barong.

The strong link between Barong and each village comes from the belief that a spirit sibling named Banas Pati Raja accompanies every Balinese child throughout life. Some writers consider this spirit a form of guardian angel, and the Banas Pati Raja spirit from every villager combines to animate Barong. Barong then guards the village, as long as everyone remembers to carry out the rituals for their spirit siblings. Other writers have described Banas Pati Raja as being the 'Lord of the Woods', and this spirit takes the form of Barong to defeat evil.

Barong stands in opposition to Rangda, the fearsome queen of the demons, represented as a witch with tangled hair, claws, and fangs. In some stories, Rangda eats corpses and even feasts on the innards of children. Barong and Rangda appear

in a range of legends, and the Barong dance recreates one of them, as described by anthropologist J Stephen Lansing. In this story, Rangda needs a child's corpse and sends her daughter Rarong to fetch one from the graveyard. Barong stumbles across the scene and, disgusted by the sight of Rarong playing with a dead baby, chases her away. Rangda storms into the graveyard to fight Barong, although he emerges from the battle triumphant.

During the dance, men try to attack Rangda with daggers, but she uses her evil magic to force them to turn their weapons on themselves. Barong lends them his magic so they stop attacking themselves and pursue Rangda as planned. Wherever dancers perform the Barong dance, the ritual re-enacts the continual battle between Rangda and Barong, symbolizing the battle between good and evil. While Barong often appears to win the battle, good and evil are actually kept in balance, rather than one defeating the other. These performances are popular with tourists, and two dancers operate the masked Barong for the rituals during holidays. Barong masks are common souvenirs, and he also appears on both postcards and adverts. There are theories that the battle is a re-enactment of an old 11th-century story from Java, in which a powerful widow terrorized the people with her evil magic. The king sent a priest to deal with her and they fought an epic battle, which the priest eventually won. The widow becomes Rangda, and the priest becomes Barong. When dancers perform this version, people are warned not to leave until the dance is finished, otherwise they might encounter the spirits of the dead on their way home.

Villages keep their Barong masks either in their death temple or in small shrines near their meeting halls. The masks have special powers, so if a disease takes hold in a village, the priest can dip the mask's beard into ordinary water, turning the water into a healing potion (even thought to cure scabies). In the village of Gianyar, the priest anointed the eyes of the Barong mask with oil and then dripped the oil onto the suffering patient. Priests also sprinkle the masks with holy water before each performance of the Barong dance.

Even in the 21st century, Barong provides protection for Bali in the form of economic help, since local artisans produce the Barong souvenirs that are so popular with tourists. Yet the 'commercial' form of the Barong dance is not the same as the sacred version, with the tourist and local dances kept separate to help preserve the Balinese culture.

Barong can also be seen as a guardian of the land, or the forest. Scholars have noted that the movements of the Barong dances often recall movements we see in nature, like trees bending in the wind or the way different animals move. This harks back to the animist origins of Barong and the dependence people had on nature. Since animism is an ancient belief system in which everything has a spirit of its own, from rocks and trees to the stars and rivers, the idea of a protective spirit taking an animal form makes sense. Animism still exists at the heart of many Indigenous cultures, and it is a worldview that not only holds the natural world as sacred, but also encourages us to see ourselves as part of the natural world, not separate from it.

The movements of the Barong dances often recall movements we see in nature, like trees bending in the wind or the way different animals move.

In the West, we're often encouraged to see the world as a source of resources to be exploited for our own gain. But while it might feel like modern technology helps to hold the darkness at bay, evil is never far away. For as long as it threatens the world with destruction and chaos, Barong remains ready to battle with Rangda. In an ever-changing world with new and distinct threats, Barong is a constant principle of all that is good, and everything we should seek to protect.

Bird Maidens

A tall, flightless bird stalks through the forest, her blue neck rearing upwards from the glossy black feathers that cover her back. With her pointed beak, scaled feet and the horn on her head, she looks almost reptilian. The cassowary pauses for a moment, before stepping out of its skin in a flurry of feathers. The young woman that stands in its place folds the skin over her arm, and disappears into the undergrowth.

The idea of a bird that transforms into a woman appears in folklore all over the world. The shapeshifting maidens most often take the form of swans, although throwing off their feathers to turn into women left them vulnerable. Nefarious men could steal these feathers, forcing them to remain in their human form and manipulating them into marriage. These toxic husbands had to keep the feather skins hidden, because if the women ever found them, they would regain their swan form and escape.

Elsewhere in the Pacific and Oceania, the enchanted maiden also takes aquatic forms, like whales, fish, and dolphins. The stories suggest human exploitation of the environment, with the men stealing what they want from the natural world without any consideration for the damage they do. In New Guinea, the legend also includes bird women who appear as cassowaries or birds of paradise, in reference to the local differences in wildlife.

These stories often try to promote a vision of women as being docile, compliant, and dutiful. The moment they rebel by regaining their skins, they're viewed as selfish for abandoning their husbands and families. Yet in these narratives outside of Europe, the bird women often stand in for the Indigenous populations harmed by colonialism. The fact that one of the New Guinea tales is titled 'A Worthless Man Married a Gorgeous Woman' tells us a lot about how people may have actually viewed these forced marriages and the men that insisted on them.

The metaphor also applies to abusive relationships of other types, with people manipulated into staying in conditions that they cannot flee without help, or communities locked in dangerous situations with powerful authorities that mean them harm. Allies need to step up and ensure that anyone trapped in such situations is allowed to be free.

Pleiades

You lie on your back, gazing up at the night sky. The cold fingers of dawn pry at the edges of the horizon so you enjoy the view of the stars before day breaks. A cluster of seven stars catches your eye, twinkling in the vast, velvety expanse of space. The longer you stare, the more you're sure you see them moving—seven lithe women dance across the sky, spreading frost in their wake across the world below.

The story of the Seven Sisters is widespread across Indigenous Australia, although variations appear in different regions. The group also has different names to reflect the differences in languages across the continent. In most versions, the Pleiades (as they're also known) were a group of sisters that traveled across the country. An old man followed them because he wanted one as a wife, even though he was from the wrong kinship group and forbidden to marry her. He shifted his form into everything from animals to trees in his efforts to snare one of the women. They could also change their shape, and they repeatedly avoided his amorous advances with their ingenious transformations into flowers or rocks.

Eventually, to escape his relentless pursuit, the sisters reached a tall hill and leapt into the sky, where they became stars. This didn't deter the old man, who chased them into the celestial realm and became, depending on the story, either a star in Orion's belt, the planet Venus, or Aldebaran, the glowing orange star that forms the eye of the Taurus bull. In other versions of the story, the sisters originally came from the sky, and the old man pursued them when they came to Earth, grabbing the youngest sister while the women were out hunting. The other six sisters ran back to their cave, their passage back to the sky, to escape. Their youngest sister fought off the old man and also reached the cave, but this explains why the seventh Pleiad is often quite difficult to see compared to the other six—she still hasn't quite caught up.

Despite the vast size of Australia and the huge portion of the night sky visible from the continent, the common focus on the Pleiades shows how important they are in the 'Dreaming'. Though the name was coined by European anthropologists, the Dreaming is the Indigenous Australian worldview, explaining where everything in the universe came from, how life appeared, and the rules everyone must follow. Creator beings made songlines, or paths, as they moved across the land and sky to create the world. Songs, paintings, and dances map the routes and the stories that

accompany them. Some of the songlines cross the territories of different groups and languages, and the stories preserve cultural knowledge about traditional law and even the way society works. Some groups performed the Pleiades legend during initiation practices for girls.

In some parts of Australia, people believed the Pleiades had visited the area when they woke up and found frost spread across their camp. The sisters are strongly linked with water and ice, and the sites named in their stories are often those where people can find water. Other stories see the sisters take the form of birds, including jays and choughs, which makes a fascinating link with the Greek myth of Halcyone, one of the Seven Sisters, who is transformed into a kingfisher after angering Hera and Zeus. The Gundungurra people of New South Wales have a version in which the old man is a magpie, and the sisters are white-winged choughs. The magpie saves one of the choughs from peril so she marries him, but the magpie turns out to be so lazy that he makes the women do all the work. Eventually, a storm approaches, and the choughs promise to strip bark from a tree to build a shelter. As she strips the bark, her sisters sing a charm and the tree grows taller until it carries her into the night sky. Her sisters follow and they all become stars.

The Australian story is a lot older than the first contact with Europeans—it could even be the oldest story in the world.

While the Pleiades are known as the Seven Sisters, there are actually over 800 stars in the cluster, which sits in the Taurus constellation. Most of the stories only concern the seven most visible stars, although most people can now only see six because Pleione and Atlas have moved closer together and look like a single star to the naked eye. The story explained the apparent movement of the stars across the night sky as they re-enacted their drama every night. We now know that it's the Earth moving, not the stars, but the story still explains the celestial events visible from Earth. The Pleiades are so important to Indigenous Australian cultures that the Pitjantjatjara Aboriginal women performed the 'Dance of the Pleiades' during the opening ceremony of the 2000 Sydney Olympics.

What's so fascinating about this myth is that there are similar variations in different cultures across the world and time periods, including Africa, Europe, Asia, Indonesia, and Indigenous North America. While some early white scholars assumed Europeans carried the Greek myth to Australia, the Australian story is a lot older than the first contact with Europeans—it could even be the oldest story in the world. The Indigenous Australian academic Munya Andrews has written about the similarities and differences between these tales. When early humans first migrated out of Africa, Pleione and Atlas would have been further apart, and easier to distinguish as separate stars. Academics suggest that this migration from a shared starting point could explain why similar stories about seven stars developed in different cultures.

Yet if we look at the Pleiades from an animist perspective, the similarity of the tales suggests that humans encounter and experience these stars (and their spirits) in complementary ways. It also encourages us to look at the elements of the natural world as friends and neighbors, rather than inert features, making our efforts to respond to the climate crisis essential to being part of a wider community.

Bunyip

Something slips through the dark water in front of you. It hauls itself onto the bank, water smoothing down its thick fur, and the moonlight gleams across its tusks. It looks like someone crossed a manatee with a horse, with added fangs and flippers. It unleashes a booming howl. Only a bunyip could make an unearthly sound like that.

The bunyip appears in the Aboriginal folklore of Australia, living in the swamps and lakes of the country's interior. Descriptions of it vary: from having the body of an ox or hippopotamus, to appearing more human or more like a manatee. The size of a cow, the bunyip also had sharp tusks, while different versions sported long fur, feathers, or scales. The bunyip could even transform its flippers into legs, making it the ultimate amphibious predator.

According to legend, the bunyip enjoyed having women or children on the menu, although this may have been a cautionary tale to warn people to stay away from dangerous water hazards, particularly at night. The bunyip was also said to roar and howl, though scholars now think this might have been the cry of the bittern, a marsh bird that makes a booming noise. Others think the stories may have come from the sounds peat bogs make when they expand and contract due to atmospheric changes.

In 1846, a bunyip skull went on display at the Australian Museum in Sydney, which prompted a sudden wave of 'confessions' from people claiming they'd seen or heard things in the river at night. Scientists later confirmed the skull was that of a horse, though it's not clear how many witnesses retracted their sightings! Then in 1934, the artist Gerald Lewers created a sculpture of the bunyip that looked more like the extinct Diprotodon. People had found fossils of this ancient grazing marsupial and sometimes thought they might be bunyips.

The bunyip is a good example of the ways colonialism has stolen and sanitized Indigenous stories. European settlers learned the story and changed its meaning as they retold it, and by the 19th century 'bunyip' had become a word that meant 'imposter'—a world away from the terrifying monster it once referred to. Even worse, at some point the bunyip switched to vegetarianism and became a popular fixture in childrens' books. This is an excellent reason to instead seek authentic stories by Indigenous storytellers so you can support their cultural work.

Moehau Man

The undergrowth shakes and the trees part, revealing a tall humanoid figure. Thick dark hair covers its entire body, and wicked claws top its bony fingers. It clutches a stone club in one hand and growls. You stay hidden. The Moehau Man's pungent odor drifts towards you and you try not to gag on the stench.

According to New Zealand folklore, the Moehau Man is an aggressive creature in the Coromandel-Moehau mountains on the North Island. The Moehau Man's name comes from the name of the highest mountain in the range. To some Māori people, the Moehau Man possibly descends from the Maero—wild men, sometimes described as giants, who lived in the forests and mountains of New Zealand. The Maero were fearsome figures who used stone clubs to batter and kill their prey, which often included humans. In Māori stories, the Maero hated the Māori for forcing them deeper into the forests.

There are seveal sightings and stories of the Moehau Man, beginning when European settlers first claimed land in the area. In 1882, locals found the decapitated, partly eaten body of a prospector near the Martha Mine in the mountains. The same year, miners found a woman's corpse in the foothills, after she'd been dragged from her home. Some blamed the Moehau Man for both deaths, though it's possible the stories of the creature were invented to dissuade prospectors from finding profitable seams. Others think the Moehau Man was actually a gorilla that escaped from a ship that docked in New Zealand in 1924.

In 1970, a newspaper article claimed the story was ultimately a hoax after a local councillor explained that the legend began as a joke. Over time, people added their own stories and superstitions, and the Moehau Man took on a life of its own. While this can happen within folklore and often creates urban legends, it doesn't explain the 19th-century sightings and stories which pre-date the newspaper article.

Cryptid fans online have noted the Moehau Man's similarity with Bigfoot and the Yeti, although the Moehau Man appears to use tools, unlike his cryptid cousins. Yet the Moehau Man remains a reminder that we don't always know what lies in the depths of the natural world, and exploiting it for resources might be a dangerous act.

Aida

A teenage girl stands beside an old baobab tree, its gnarled branches reaching towards the sky in greeting. Long hair tumbles down her back and she mimics the tree's stance as she calls out to the clouds. Large, glistening raindrops begin to fall to the ground, throwing up puffs of dust where they land. You notice in the distance that there is one area where the rain doesn't fall, and you realize this can only be Aida.

Literary scholar Omar Sougou explains that many African folktales depict women as voiceless or invisible, while men are dominant and hold all the authority. Yet the tale of Aida from Senegal bucks this trend, showing us a worthwhile heroine who fights for equality within a system that doesn't recognize her worth. The story overturns typical social attitudes in the face of justice, explaining its popularity well into the 21st century.

A woman named Famata is pregnant in a land known as Tarokoro, but there's just one problem: the regime kills baby girls and their mothers since they only want boys, and Famata is expecting a daughter. The new mother escapes the planned femicide and hides in the trunk of an old baobab tree, where she gives birth to a baby girl, who she names Aida.

Aida grows up to be a beautiful young woman, discovering an awesome power as she gets older—she can control the rains with her prayers, and she asks God to make sure the rains fall everywhere except Tarokoro, causing severe droughts, which damage the crops. The people of the land slowly starve and, eventually, the king sends out a spy to find out the cause of the problem. He spots Aida and soon realizes she is the reason the rains won't fall in the kingdom. The king sends for her and begs to know what her issue is with Tarokoro.

Aida rails on him, berating him for his sexist policy, and demands to know why he murders baby girls at birth. The king explains they consider boys to be productive, unlike girls who they see as passive consumers. Aida argues with him that she has learned to do everything the boys can do, purely to survive, and the king agrees to end the policy. Equality comes to Tarokoro so Aida allows the rains to return. (It's unclear if the king actually agrees with Aida, or agrees purely to

get her to allow the rain to fall, but whatever his reasons, Aida wins her case.)

The story withholds the king's reason for killing the baby girls until Aida's royal audience, and this places us in Aida's position. We know as much (or as little) as she does, and so her rage at a deeply unfair practice feels more real and immediate. We're also encouraged to side with Aida since the story is named after her. Crucially, Sougou explains that the story also lacks a traditional hero: no one defeats Aida or forces her to make the rains return. Only Aida has the power over the rains, and only Aida can change her actions, making her both the heroine and the villain of the story rolled into one.

Only Aida has the power over the rains, and only Aida can change her actions, making her both the heroine and the villain of the story rolled into one.

This tale is unusual because it links Aida with a magical power over the rains, but she isn't associated with witchcraft, an art more often practised by mature women. Her age may be partly the reason that she isn't branded a witch, since she's only a teenager in the story. She isn't even painted as evil, but rather she's shown as angry at a regime that doesn't recognize her valid existence. Aida becomes an avenger of slain mothers and baby girls, although she doesn't use her power to protect them. Instead, she uses her audience with the king to secure their future by successfully arguing that they're just as useful as boys.

Aida's prayers for the rain to avoid Tarokoro are her only real weapon, though the power ultimately comes from her prayers to God, after she explains that the men of Tarokoro murder their mothers and baby girls. Though God's decision to withhold rain from the region definitely feels like tacit support for Aida's cause!

Women have been associated with water in folktales for centuries—just look at the number of nymphs, spirits, and goddesses of water. Water is life giving, shown through the importance of the rain, but it can also be destructive, manifesting as flash floods or tsunamis. The absence of rain mirrors the murder of the mothers, whose life-giving abilities are taken away. The king's belief that women aren't producers is, of course, somewhat ironic, given their role in the reproductive process.

It's also important to know this folktale was collected from young Senegalese women working as housemaids, who performed a range of tales for their friends. Performing folktales was a way for these urban girls to stay connected to their rural families, but it's also noteworthy that the story captures the strength, ingenuity, and bravery of women. Aida's bold address to the king, in which she ignores royal protocol and demands answers, is an excellent example of speaking truth to power. Perhaps the girls could see a little of themselves in Aida and could inspire them to be strong and independent too.

Anansi

A tall man barters with a stallholder in a market over juicy fresh fruit. The man holds four of his six arms behind his back in a bid to appear more human. But you listen to the bartering and you can tell this is no mere mortal. Only Anansi could get a deal as good as this, while making the stallholder think they have the upper hand. He takes his fruit, pops a berry into his mouth, and winks at you as he walks away.

Kwaku Anansi, or Anansi for short, hails from Ghana, although his influence spreads across West Africa to the Caribbean and the American South. 'Anansi' comes from the Twi language, where the word 'ananse' means spider. Even in Africa, depictions of Anansi vary, although in many images he appears as an eight-limbed man. In some stories, he can shapeshift between a human form and that of a spider, or he appears as a spider with a man's face.

This spider god is the quintessential trickster, using his wits to overcome his far more powerful opponents. In one tale, Anansi digs a hole to trap a fierce leopard and when the cat is caught, Anansi further traps it by wrapping its paws in spiderwebs. Some of his exploits almost defy belief, which inspired a new word in the language of the Akan people, 'Anansesem', which describes incredible stories that seem almost unbelievable. He also acts as a go-between for humanity and Nyame, the supreme sky god in the mythology of the Akan. As a trickster, Anansi can move between the spiritual and physical worlds, an ability he has in common with other African tricksters.

The tales are part of a rich oral storytelling tradition that sees stories used as vehicles to pass on valuable information.

Yet there's a moral to every story and he often faces the consequences of his devious actions. In one, Anansi grudgingly agrees to share his meal with the turtle, although he schemes to keep it for himself. He invents a series of reasons why the turtle must keep leaving the table, and by the time the turtle gets back, Anansi has

eaten almost all of the food. The poor turtle leaves
hungry, but turns the tables on Anansi when the spider asks to
share a meal at the turtle's underwater house, and the trickster
goes hungry.

The tales are part of a rich oral storytelling tradition that sees stories used as vehicles
to pass on valuable information, such as ways to behave to hold a community
together. Verona Spence-Adofo writes about the importance of Anansi tales for
sharing wisdom, hiding complexity behind their apparent simplicity. After all,
Anansi is often greedy and inconsiderate towards others, yet his stories also show
the importance of forward planning, careful decision making, and strategy. Anansi
stories are so important that one of them even sees him crowned as King of All
Wisdom Narratives after undertaking a series of apparently impossible tasks.

He is an ambiguous figure, representing both good qualities, like quick thinking and
intelligence, and less desirable traits, like selfishness. It's a useful reminder that we
all possess qualities that are both admirable and problematic, but we have the ability
to choose how to act. Anansi isn't a bad figure, and some legends describe how he
taught humanity to write, hunt, and farm.

As a spider, Anansi embodies creativity, independence, practicality, and flexibility.
A spider's web can break, but the spider can set up a new one within hours. In the
same way, Anansi can change his strategy as the situation dictates. Spiders can also
snare prey that is much larger than them in their webs, reflecting Anansi's ability to
best creatures that would otherwise overcome him in power and size.

It is this aspect of his character, the ability to outwit those who could crush him if
they wanted to, that becomes important to his appearance in lore outside of Africa.
Enslaved people carried tales of Anansi to the Caribbean and North America, where
he made an appearance in folklore. Tales of his exploits proved particularly popular
in Jamaica and, in the 1920s, Martha Warren Beckwith collected enough
Jamaican Anansi stories to fill a book and preserve the tales for posterity.

He's become a popular fixture in contemporary pop culture,
from *Sesame Street* to Neil Gaiman's *American Gods*, in
which Anansi appears as Mr Nancy. Other scholars
have noted the similarities between Anansi and
the Marvel superhero Spider-Man. Anansi
even appeared in one of the comic's

storylines, while a series in 2003 described Anansi as the original Spider-Man on Earth in an alternate universe. In 1943, the 81st West African Division, who fought on the Allied side in World War II, took the inspiration for their tarantula emblem from Anansi.

Scholars have also discussed the similarity between Anansi stories and tales of Br'er Rabbit from the American South. Both figures are more than mere tricksters; they are revolutionaries. They symbolize resistance against oppression, and where brute force isn't an option, these figures use their brains to undermine tyrannical regimes. Both Anansi and Br'er Rabbit came to represent hope for enslaved people who could likewise use their wits to challenge their brutal overseers. But while Br'er Rabbit was sanitized and turned into a twee, nostalgic joker by the white folklorists who collected the stories, Anansi's trickery and cunning lives on through his legends even now.

Yumboes

A host of tiny figures dance in a circle, their dainty feet barely touching the earth. Their pearly skin almost glows in the moonlight. Silver hair streams behind them. Their singing drifts towards you on the night air. The scent of freshly roasted fish plays on the sea breeze.

These are the yumboes. They're described as a type of fairy, part of the Wolof mythology of Senegal, West Africa. The yumboes live on Gorée Island, near the capital of Dakar. According to early lore, they're two feet (60 cm) tall, have silver hair, and white skin. They may be the spirits of the dead, since they wear the same dress as the nearby humans. The Yumboes enjoy dancing under moonlight and host sumptuous feasts. Their servants are invisible, except for their hands and feet. The yumboes are fond of fish and corn; while they catch the former themselves, they steal the latter from humans. They also steal flames from the fires lit by people and use these to light their own fires, giving them somewhere to roast the fish.

The yumboes are thought to entertain humans in their underground home. One 19th-century story claims that they often host Europeans, though no first-hand accounts of these meetings appear to exist. It's worth noting that Gorée Island was the African coast's largest slave-trading center, perhaps explaining the insertion of Europeans into the yumboes' story.

It's difficult to know what to make of the yumboes. Most information about them comes from a single source—*The Fairy Mythology*, by Thomas Keightley, published in 1828. Keightley was an Irish folklorist who collected tales of fairies from around the world. He heard the yumboes lore from a woman who spent her childhood on Gorée Island. She, in turn, got the stories from her Wolof maid. Keightley noted the similarity between the yumboes and European fairies, such as their human-like behavior, underground home, and food theft.

Despite a penchant for theft, the yumboes seem to be friendly spirits, fond of humans and able to share space with them. Largely benevolent, the yumboes show how beliefs can reappear across spaces, times, and cultures. Their role as spirits of the dead is mostly peaceful, and their co-existence with humans is mischievous rather than malicious.

Mamlambo

Moonlight casts a silver glow across the surface of the river. The scene is peaceful and serene. A flicker of movement disturbs the smooth water. A creature cuts its way upstream, undulating through the river. The moonlight highlights the shimmering edges of its scales. It reaches the bank and hauls itself out, shedding its reptilian skin and leaving a beautiful woman in its place. Her hair shines like liquid silver in the night.

This is the mamlambo, associated with water in South Africa and sometimes described as a 'river goddess'. In Xhosa, 'mamlambo' means 'mother of the river'. The mamlambo is often thought of as female, although anthropologists have collected stories that also depict the mamlambo as male.

Accounts usually describe her as a snake, although in these stories she is actually a shapeshifter. She also sometimes appears as a mermaid or simply a beautiful woman. In other stories, the mamlambo is also said to have the head of a snake, short legs, the body of a crocodile, and glowing green eyes. She's a brutal hunter, alleged to suck out the brains of her victims when she kills them. In 1997, eyewitnesses claimed they saw a monster in the Mzintlava River, South Africa. They described it as being half-horse, half-fish. Stories claim the creature killed up to nine people in the river, though there is no evidence of this. Some people pointed out that the electric catfish can kill with its electric shocks, which may help to provide an explanation.

But there's more to the mamlambo than a river-dwelling snake goddess. In some stories, the mamlambo is more of a creature than a deity. Witches might snare a mamlambo to be their familiar. They'd catch one in a bottle, in which it looked like a root that glowed in the dark. As it grew, it turned into a snake covered with hair, with eyes like diamonds. The witch hid the mamlambo during the day. At night, it turned into a white person with silver hair and became the witch's lover.

The mamlambo brought a lot of money to the witch in return for their offerings of chicken and beef (and sometimes, on a slightly more sinister note, human blood). In some stories, people accuse their richer neighbors of having a mamlambo. This brings class envy into the stories, where accusations are motivated by wealth.

There is always a strong link between a witch and their familiar, and the mamlambo stories tell of the witch and mamlambo being able to trade forms. Such a link meant that injuring or killing the river goddess would injure or kill the witch. This is common to witch stories all over the world, where a plucky hero injures a suspicious animal. The next day, someone finds that one of the community has a corresponding injury on their body.

Western capitalism collides with African traditions in a devastating way, creating a ravenous monster who can bring wealth, but sucks the lifeblood out of whatever it encounters.

But having a mamlambo as a familiar was a toxic relationship. They were very possessive of their human, and would attack their spouse if they ever married (a predicament that might condemn the witch to eternal singledom). If a witch couldn't please the mamlambo with sacrifices and offerings, it killed them. Warnings abound that the witch must sacrifice those closest to them to keep the mamlambo happy—if they didn't, the mamlambo would wreak havoc on their family. Sacrificing loved ones to get what you want says as much about the witch and their desire as it does the mamlambo.

Some stories stress the difference between the male and female mamlambo. A male mamlambo will make his owner wealthy and make others poor. This makes the male a better choice if your end goal is money or power. A female mamlambo eats anything with a blood supply—an ideal choice if you want to inflict harm on others!

As with most folktales, interpretations aren't always so clearcut. There are other stories of those seeking wealth who choose the female mamlambo to help them. Her price is his sexual fidelity and she may even wear out her unfortunate human lover. In these tales, her immense sexual appetite leaves him incapable of satisfying his human wife. The marriage ends in divorce, rather than death, but the mamlambo owner still destroys something in his life to increase his wealth.

Some scholars think the mamlambo
is a reasonably new spirit in southern
Africa, most often gendered as female.
When referred to as a goddess, she seems to have
evolved out of social, economic, and political processes. The fact she appears as a
pale-skinned woman wearing Western clothes becomes significant: it shows how
the mamlambo may come from a desire for material success in Western terms.
Western capitalism collides with African traditions in a devastating way, creating
a ravenous monster who can bring wealth, but sucks the lifeblood out of whatever
it encounters. We could argue that capitalism itself does this, offering the promise
of wealth but at the expense of a person's health or wellbeing—just look at the
burnout that so often accompanies 'hustle culture'.

The mamlambo also comes from a conflict between African beliefs and Western
ideas. Snakes in traditions around the world are often benevolent or positive figures,
representing renewal and rebirth. In ancient Egypt, the snake goddess Wadjet was
considered the protector of both Egypt and the pharoahs, retaining her important
place even as the popularity of other gods waxed and waned. A snake even wraps
itself around the Rod of Asclepius, the international symbol of healing, through its
association with the ancient Greek god of medicine, Asclepius. But the mamlambo
brings with her the darker side of snakes—not through their venomous nature, but
rather the Christian association of snakes with evil thanks to temptation; here
shown as the allure of money and material possessions. While the stories focus on
the sexual allure of the female mamlambo, many of the perils come from the owner's
intense desire for wealth. It's worth remembering that the Bible doesn't say money
is the root of all evil, but rather the love of money that causes the problem.

Impundulu

A large white bird flies above you, its red legs tucked up against its body. Crashes of thunder roll around the sky as it beats its red wings. Without warning, it dives towards the ground. Lightning tears open the sky in response.

The impundulu ('lightning bird') appears in South African folklore. You can find it in tales from the Pondo, the Zulu, and the Xhosa tribes. They are dangerous creatures, and stories say that shamans tried to find their nests so they could break the eggs, stopping more impumdulus from hatching. Since the birds enjoy drinking milk, people would also poison milk to kill them. Others say the only way to kill the impundulu is to strike it through the flash of lightning that accompanied it.

According to the legends, the impundulu can be a witch's familiar. A helpful companion, it attacks on command, and some say it even drinks human blood. When they're not busy assisting the witches, these vampiric birds might abduct children.

In some legends, the bird can adopt human form, appearing as an attractive young man so it can seduce young women. If an impundulu got a woman pregnant, she would give birth to birds. Like several other seductive folk villains, from the mamlambo (page 156) to boco encantado (page 170), the impundulu often appears in Western clothes—which says a lot about the Western threat to community that these figures represent. Other legends say that if an impundulu takes on a human appearance, only women can see its real bird form. This could reflect the sad truth that women must be more vigilant about the risks posed by strangers. Here, the impundulu becomes a cautionary tale. Tellers code warnings about our fears into stories to make these warnings easier to pass on, explaining why the impundulu seems to appear in so many different dark tales.

Writers in the 1930s, such as the scholar of Bantu languages Alice Werner, were somewhat disparaging about the impundulu folklore, scoffing at the idea that birds could bring lightning. But the stories provide a helpful explanation of natural phenomena, including both lightning and meteorite strikes. There is also a possibility that the bird helped to explain diseases; if you developed tuberculosis, people said the impundulu had stolen your breath. The impundulu gives us a way to explore the dangers posed by extreme weather, disease, and predatory men.

Mami Wata

A beautiful woman swims through crystal clear water, her long hair streaming behind her. Light dances along the glittering scales of her fishtail. You blink, and she changes form. Now she stands before you, a glorious Black woman holding aloft a mighty snake in one hand. The snake coils its tail around her other hand. She holds your gaze and you kneel, overwhelmed by her awesome presence.

Both of these representations belong to the same figure: Mami Wata. Her name refers both to a single deity, and a group of water spirits, known as mami watas. She is associated with snakes, sometimes pictured holding a gigantic snake. Other images show her as a mermaid with long, flowing hair.

People disagree about where her name comes from. Some scholars say it comes from pidgin English, a language developed in Africa to support communication with other nations. Other writers point to its roots in early Ethiopian languages, showing that Mami Wata belief pre-dates European involvement in Africa. But not all writers think Mami Wata is African in origin. In one theory, Mami Wata came from the Caribbean and people brought her worship to Africa. In another, Mami Wata is a new name for an existing group of ancient spirits. For others, images of Hindu deities and European mermaids influenced Mami Wata's appearance. Yet other writers have found evidence of Mami Wata in African myths that are over 4,000 years old. The coast of Guinea provides a likely location for her original worship.

Wherever she originated, enslaved people carried her cult to the Americas during the slave trade. Some scholars think Yemanjá, worshipped in South America, is another form of Mami Wata. Both are fond of luxurious gifts and associated with mirrors and combs—and the surface of a mirror reminds us of the reflective nature of water.

Mami Wata is incredibly beautiful, often linked with fertility and sex. Though 'Mami' often translates as 'Mother', Mami Wata doesn't have any children. Instead, she's sometimes considered a protector of mothers, and able to cure infertility. In other stories, she causes infertility as a punishment for gorgeous women whose beauty makes them arrogant, reversing the condition when the women pay devotion to her.

She looks after her worshippers by providing healing for devotees who have come to her for help in difficult times. She can also talk to devotees through dreams, telling them what they need to do for her. There are more recent reports of Mami Wata causing a crisis in peoples' lives, and then reversing this once they learned of her and worshipped her.

Mami Wata is also the mother and guardian of water. In some places, people avoid approaching seas or lakes on given days to give Mami Wata a break from her guardianship duties. She's also believed to help the descendants of enslaved people reconnect with their ancestral waters: in some tales, she even capsizes ships taking enslaved people to the Americas.

Be wary of swimming in rivers or the sea; sometimes people in the water are taken on a spiritual journey to Mami Wata's underwater home. Allegedly, she returns the people that survive the journey to the human world, where they enjoy more wealth and success after the encounter. In recent tales, wealth and success can come in the form of a career boost.

She stands before you, a glorious Black woman holding aloft a mighty snake in one hand. She holds your gaze and you kneel, overwhelmed by her awesome presence.

Wealth is a common association with Mami Wata. She can make you rich, but you must enter a relationship with her first. Men that reject her, or are unfaithful to her, can find themselves thrown into poverty. In some stories, she will only give men more wealth if they become her faithful lovers, and give up the opportunity to have children with their human partners. It's possible this idea came from the childless Europeans encountered by West Africans, who had wealth and power, but no family. Some writers think colonialism twisted local beliefs about making pacts with the spirit world. In this case, you made a pact with Mami Wata to gain wealth. These beliefs became more common as Western money systems wreaked havoc on local economies, focusing on a way to 'get' wealth, rather than inheriting or earning it.

Yet those who seek wealth from Mami Wata must still pay for it, one way or another. For some, they do so through worship and devotion, making this a positive, joyful, and uplifting experience. In other stories, they sacrifice their independence or the children they'll never have. Where they do receive wealth, it's not always in monetary terms, but often as spiritual healing. Personifying the awesome power of water, Mami Wata reminds us that the environment can both give and take away. Instead of only enjoying her benevolence, we should 'give back' to keep everything in balance—and remember that we need the natural world more than it needs us.

Zankallala

The Zankallala appears at the side of the trail. He is small—around six inches high—and he rides a jerboa, a hopping desert rodent, as though it were a mighty steed. A bee swarm clings to his head and he carries a stiffened snake as a walking stick.

The Zankallala is a trickster figure found in the folklore of the Hausa people, an ethnic group from West and Central Africa. His unusual appearance makes him stand out among other creatures: he may be small in stature, but he's big in charisma and presence (a powerful reminder that size doesn't matter!). Hosts of birds follow the Zankallala to sing his praises, and on occasion, they attack whichever enemies he encounters. He can also be helpful to humans, if the fancy takes him, making him an unpredictable ally.

In one traditional story, a dodo chases a boy along the riverbank. (If this doesn't seem scary enough, bear in mind that the dodo was sometimes called the "swallower of men".) The boy meets the Zankallala and explains that the dodo is chasing him. The Zankallala tells him not to fear. The dodo arrives and demands that he hand over the boy. The Zankallala feigns ignorance so the dodo threatens him: if the Zankallala won't hand over the boy, then he'll eat the Zankallala instead. When the Zankallala still refuses to hand over the boy, the dodo swallows him whole. The Zankallala bursts free unharmed from the dodo's stomach. The second time the dodo swallows him, he bursts out of the dodo's back. By the third time, the Zankallala bursts out of the dodo's head, and it drops dead on the spot. The boy escapes, and the birds sing the Zankallala's praises for outwitting the dodo.

Other variations of the story exist, with witches and snakes taking on the role of villain. In each of these stories, the Zankallala represents a quintessential trickster figure. Appearing in cultures around the world, the trickster is an ancient archetype, ultimately representing chaos and unpredictability; you never know whether the trickster will help or hinder you. Ironically, the one thing people could rely on the trickster to do was to be unreliable! Yet tricksters are also subversive figures. In this 'David and Goliath' tale, the tiny Zankallala overturns power dynamics by beating the larger monster using wits and courage, rather than brute strength. It's a welcome antidote from the over-reliance on the rescuing Hero and Warrior archetypes present in other tales.

Boto Encantado

A tall, handsome man makes his way through the crowd at a busy bar. He wears white clothing and a hat, tipped at a jaunty angle. The man pauses to dance for a moment with a woman in the crowd. Another woman grabs his hand and pulls him towards the bar. He can't resist her, since he's the boto encantado, and he loves both women and dancing.

The boto is a pink river dolphin that lives in the Amazon river, famous for scything through the water with grace and agility. Their mesmerizing speed may have led people to consider them as having supernatural qualities.

'Encantado' (meaning 'charmed' in Portuguese) refers to the magical nature of this slippery folk character. At night, the pink dolphin turns into a handsome white man who enjoys dancing. While he's on land, he seduces women, but he returns to the river before dawn and swims away in his dolphin form. And we thought the dangers of Tinder were bad enough…

Descriptions of the boto stress how attractive he is, but there is a way to avoid his charms: ask him to take off his hat. His breathing hole doesn't disappear when he changes form so if he has one on the top of his head, he's a boto.

Some extreme stories describe the botos paralyzing humans to have sex with them, then turning back into a dolphin after committing rape. The encounter can bring on illness or even death for the victim. Their soul becomes the dolphin's partner without the person ever giving consent, their enforced bond a tragic symbol of the rape victim's ongoing trauma.

Anthropologist Mark A Cravalho collected a story from a teenager in the Middle Amazon. One night, she had a fight with her boyfriend. She invited him over the next night, but he called for her to come outside so they could talk. She thought this was strange since he didn't normally do this when he came by, and, feeling it was too late for a conversation, she sent him away. When her boyfriend arrived the next day, he insisted he hadn't dropped by the night before. The girl became unable to move, and a local healer diagnosed the problem: a dolphin had bewitched her.

In another story collected by Cravalho, a male boto appeared at parties, where he drank a lot of beer. He never paid for his drinks, leading the bartender to send some men after him. They shot at him so he jumped into the water, where he transformed back into a dolphin. But the shot proved fatal, and the dead boto washed up on the shore. A girl wanted to see the body and, despite her mother's refusal, she went along. After turning the body over, the girl developed a headache and a fever. The girl soon died, and a local medium explained that the boto had stolen her shadow when she touched his body. He'd pulled her soul into death to join him.

'Encantado' (meaning 'charmed' in Portuguese) refers to the magical nature of this slippery folk character.

Since the boto enjoys sex so much, some say that any child of doubtful paternity is a child of the boto. This type of story isn't restricted to the Amazon. In medieval Europe, women might claim an incubus fathered their illegitimate child. The incubus shares a lot of characteristics with the boto encantado, including the ability to paralyze a human lover at night.

This shows the mixing of European, Indigenous and African ideas in the Amazon. But this mixing of traditions also hides a much darker history. Journalist Andriolli Costa explains that the stories of the boto date back to the 18th century, emerging when the Portuguese seized Brazil using violence. The original boto story was a warning about the dangers posed by the white colonizers. These colonizers destroyed communities and often left the local women pregnant with their children.

Folklorists also think that, even now, the stories continue as a warning against strangers in small or remote communities. Strangers who enjoy partying might be suspicious, especially if they pursue local women while they do so. That the boto always becomes a white man is very telling; it warns small communities of the dangers Europeans pose to their way of life, and also that white men feel entitled to the attention of local women. Read in this light, the boto encantado becomes a cautionary tale for the community as a whole.

The boto encantado story relies on outdated gender stereotypes. While stories of a female boto do exist, they're so often eclipsed by tales of the male boto. The male boto only seeks female partners, reinforcing the cultural primacy of straight relationships and ignoring the possibility of other partnerships. It also dictates female behaviour, since women who meet handsome strangers in bars have to be careful how they handle the situation. The boto carries no responsibility for his actions, placing sole responsibility for the outcome on the woman in a typical case of victim-blaming. The stories in which women meet the boto in a bar and choose to enjoy his company at least raise the possibility of female agency, although the stories in which unconsenting women find themselves bewitched by dolphins employing manipulative tactics are alarming in their portrayal of male sexual entitlement. A "boto will be a boto" sentiment reflects the troubling "boys will be boys" idea that is so often wheeled out as an excuse for rape or sexual assault.

So the boto is born out of the violence and destruction of colonization, but today the story is still used as a dark fig leaf. Some men in isolated communities might use the boto encantado to explain a sudden, otherwise unexplained pregnancy in cases of incest or rape, and the boto becomes a convenient excuse to hide their predatory behavior. The children born of abusive encounters become "children of the boto." Where the boto story first warned people about outsiders, now it also warns about those within the family who mean harm. This shows the darker side of folklore, in which a useful cautionary tale can be repurposed by an abuser to absolve them of their actions. It's also a reminder that we sometimes need to look beyond the surface of a seemingly cute or quaint folktale to see what horrors truly lurk beneath.

Mapinguari

An enormous creature forces through the undergrowth in the Amazon jungle. It walks on all fours, its long, curling claws pressing into the soil, heavy enough to crush tree roots beneath its feet as it walks. The beast hauls itself up, standing over seven feet tall. But you don't quite notice its immense height. No, you stare at the grinning maw on its stomach, a mouth that could swallow you whole in a heartbeat.

It's hardly surprising the Mapinguari is such a popular cryptid. Sightings aren't rare, running into the hundreds. Some stories feature a humanoid figure, covered in thick hair with only one eye. Other stories claim it has a second mouth in the stomach, echoing Christian art that showed the Devil with a second mouth in his abdomen.

The Mapinguari is sometimes thought to have a magical origin story. In these legends, a shaman in the Amazon learned how to become immortal. This angered the gods (as is often the case when a plucky human oversteps the boundaries of mortal life), and they turned him into a Mapinguari as a punishment. But the more plausible explanation lies in an ancient animal species. The Megatherium, part of the ground sloth family, lived in the Amazon rainforest until 12,000 years ago. The most famous species was the *M. americanum*, which was the size of an elephant. Some people think the Mapinguari is one of these animals that somehow survived extinction and developed a taste for meat. The Mapinguari supposedly has an enormous appetite for cattle, explaining the loss of any missing livestock among farmers who have moved into deforested areas of the jungle.

Others think it is more likely that the Mapinguari refers to a surviving folk memory of the animal. Scientists have explored the forest to see if the sightings could be real, but they found no proof the Mapinguari exists. Believers say the forest is large enough to hide the creature.

It's interesting that the Mapinguari never injures or attacks humans in the forest. Instead, witnesses encounter its vile smell, so strong it can knock people unconscious. More recently, online articles have described the Mapinguari as a forest protector, driving off human invaders with its size and stench. These newer claims may be a result of a greater awareness of threats to the Amazon, where the Mapinguari rises as a sloth-like avenger of the jungle.

Yemanjá

A full moon hangs low over a calm sea. Its light glitters across the waters lapping at the beach. A beautiful woman emerges from the gentle waves. She holds her arms outstretched and her palms facing the night sky above. Black hair falls around her shoulders and she wears a star on her forehead.

This is Yemanjá, Queen of the Ocean. Her name comes from the Yoruban phrase, 'YéYé Omó Ejá', which means, 'Mother whose children are fish'.

She comes from West Africa, mother of the Orishas in the Yoruba religion. The Orishas are often thought of as deities, though they transcend the way we think of gods in the West. They can personify natural forces, or can also be ancestors and divine beings that pre-date humanity.

In Yemanja's homeland, she is the patron deity of the rivers. Enslaved people brought her with them to Brazil where she became the goddess of the sea, or Queen of the Ocean. She is the patron of sailors, shipwreck survivors and fishermen, helping to protect their boats from capsizing.

Yemanjá is also a goddess of moonlight. She is protective (especially of women), nurturing, and cures female infertility. In one myth, she gave birth to the first humans. The rivers and streams came from the flood caused when her waters broke. Life began with Yemanjá, so she's seen as a creator goddess.

She's usually calm, but destructive if she loses her temper, which helps to explain violent storms at sea or turbulent rivers. Some images show her as a mermaid and folk art from her major centers of worship includes handmade ceramic mermaids.

In Brazil, she's also part of the Umbanda and Candomblé traditions, among others. Umbanda grew out of African rituals, infused with Catholicism and Indigenous traditions. Candomblé also combines West African traditions and Catholicism. When the colonial authorities banned traditional African religions and forced them to practice Catholicism, enslaved people developed these traditions to continue their practices in secret. It is for this reason that Yemanjá is often syncretized with the Virgin Mary. This is less because of their shared qualities, and more because of

Brazilian history. By replacing their Orishas with saints, people could continue their practices away from repressive eyes.

On 2 February, Candomblé followers celebrate Yemanjá in Salvador. She shares this day with Nossa Senhora dos Navegantes, or Our Lady of Seafaring. This is one of the titles given to the Virgin Mary, and Portuguese sailors venerate this aspect of Mary to protect them during storms. Yemanjá is also thought to protect those who need to travel by boat.

In some stories, Yemanjá punishes humanity for our misuse of nature. Her strong links with water are also an urgent reminder of the importance of water management.

During the festival, people dress in white and go to her shrine in Rio Vermelho at dawn to leave offerings of flowers, perfume, combs, and jewelry. Local fishermen take the offerings out to sea and people dance well into the night. Other followers make temporary shrines on the shore and make their offerings there, sometimes sending their benefactions out to sea on small boats. If your gift washes up on shore, it's said Yemanjá has rejected the offering, but if it makes it out to sea, then she has accepted it. In the past, followers held these rituals in secret. But some writers have noted that the practices became more public in 1923, after a period of especially poor fishing. Desperate fisherman left offerings for Yemanjá, asking her for better catches. People watched what they did and the ritual caught on.

In Rio de Janeiro, Brazilians celebrate Yemanjá on New Year's Eve. People of different religious backgrounds dress in white and gather on the beach to throw white flowers into the sea. Others leave offerings of floating candles. Those leaving offerings hope Yemanjá will grant their wishes in the new year. Jumping over the first seven waves is also a popular way to celebrate Yemanjá, and people make a different request for each wave they jump.

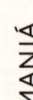

Some writers, like Carlotta Trippa and Naiara Yumiko, note the problem with whitewashing Yemanjá. Many souvenirs now depict her as a white woman, ignoring her Yoruban roots. This white-washed image of her only dates to the 1950s, when an Umbanda follower's vision of her as a white woman took hold. Important work is being done to help explore other images of Yemanjá that honor her African ancestry, and she's a popular subject for artists who want to center her Yoruban heritage.

Yemanjá personifies the ocean. The fishermen petitioning her for a good catch during hard times shows us how important nature is for our survival. In some stories, she punishes humanity for its misuse of nature. Her strong links with water are also an urgent reminder of the importance of water management. In the face of extreme drought and flash flooding, the global need for safe water supplies becomes ever more important.

Her role as a powerful goddess also makes her an important figure for those who identify as women. She represents motherhood, yet some writers stress that Yemanjá also represents qualities associated with motherhood. Those qualities, like empathy and caring for others, aren't restricted only to mothers. Caring for our environment is a wonderful way to honor the great Yemanjá.

Huayramama

A giant snake ripples through the air above the rainforest, its coils undulating as it moves. This is no ordinary snake, since it gazes down at the world with the face of an old woman. Her long hair streams behind her in the wind as she moves—the wind that she controls. This is Huayramama, the Snake Mother of the Wind. According to the legends, the Peruvian Amazon is home to three ancient snake deities: Sachamama, the Mother of the Forest, is a boa constrictor; Yakumama, the Mother of All Water Beings, is an anaconda; Huayramama is a giant boa.

The stories call Huayramama the Guardian of the Air. She gives the power to control the weather to benevolent healers and shamans, but they must prove themselves to her first. She's also called the Daughter of the Wind Tree, thought to be the huaira caspi tree.

One tale explores the story of a healer named Don Emilio Shuña. After fasting and drinking special brews, he gained mastery over the earth. But he wanted power over other elements, too. Don Emilio drank tea from the huaira caspi tree for nine days. Huayramama appeared in the sky and asked what he wanted. He made his wish: the ability to control the wind and rain. Huayramama agreed, giving him the ability to control the weather. Don Emilio used his power only for good. He brought rain to help people manage their crops. The rain also kept the rivers flowing high to make fishing easier. He could even hold off the rain when children wanted to play outside. From time to time, Huayramama strengthened his powers by touching his head. When he died, his community buried him beneath the huaira caspi tree. Trained shamans still use the huaira caspi tree in plant medicine.

In the stories, Huayramama embodies the natural world. Her ability to grant powers to worthy humans shows how humans and nature can work together. Only by following her rules and observing the proper rites can Don Emilio have his wish granted. We can get the most out of our relationship with nature by treating it with respect. Huayramama becomes an important figure for those who want to preserve the environment. She represents the balance between humans and nature. Yet she also represents the peril caused by adverse weather, something we're already seeing the effects of through the climate crisis.

La Madre Monte

Through a gap in the trees, you glimpse a tall, elegant woman with long hands. She is clad in moss and leaves that cover her body. When she smiles, you see her large teeth, though a tangle of vines and plants often falls across her face. Her large, glowing eyes stare straight at you.

Let me introduce you to La Madre Monte, a popular figure in Colombia. Her name means Mother Mountain, and she's considered Mistress of the Animals. The roots of her stories lie in the Indigenous cultures of the Antioquia and the Atrato regions. Descriptions of her vary, with some stories describing the vine-laden hat that hides her face. In some tales, she is an old woman; her face the color of ash, with red eyes and bone hands.

She makes her home in the jungles and the mountains. In the stories from the Antioquia and Caldas regions, she lives in swamps that feed streams. In other stories, she lives in great ravines among the ancient stones. Wherever she resides, sightings of her usually cluster around thickets or bushes in the forest. People report hearing La Madre Monte on stormy nights as her ghastly screams and groans echo amid the maelstrom outside. It's not surprising her cries coincide with storms, since she rules the wind and rain. These are frightening times for locals since the storms might ruin their crops.

La Madre Monte avenges people when their lands are stolen by others, making her a powerful symbol for those who have suffered at the hands of colonialism.

Despite this scary introduction, La Madre Monte is also a guardian figure. She cares for the forests, protecting the trees, plants, and animals within them. If humans venture into her territory, she manipulates the forest around them so they get lost. The path might disappear beneath vegetation that wasn't there a moment ago. Early darkness might descend, forcing them to turn around and head back the way they

came. She might even make someone so dizzy that they just need to rest for a while... and they wake up several hours later with absolutely no idea where they are.

Some versions of her legend say she targets humans who intend to destroy the forest. Woodcutters might hear screams and fear the wrath of La Madre Monte while felling trees. She also avenges people when their lands are stolen by others, making her a powerful symbol for those who have suffered at the hands of colonialism. La Madre Monte is no fan of those that overstep boundaries or take more than is their fair share. When she unleashes her wrath, she can cause devastating storms and floods.

Nature is always greater than us. In some legends, humans downstream get sick when La Madre Monte washes her hair in the river.

Yet she also picks off other human invaders, disappearing unfaithful men, and those prone to mischief if they wander into her jungle. Even vagrants who cross her path can end up lost or disorientated in the forest. If children venture into her home, La Madre Monte hides them behind waterfalls so their parents never see them again. This becomes a cautionary tale against letting children wander unsupervised. Strangely, there are few tales that explain what becomes of women who enter the forest.

You needn't go into the forest unprotected. Some say that you can carry a blessed talisman and cabalonga seeds to ward off La Madre Monte, while others say tobacco smoke keeps her away. If you encounter La Madre Monte, legend recommends insulting her to drive her away. There's even an instruction to whip her, if you can. This feels like an unsuccessful attempt to bring nature to heel.

Yet nature is always greater than us. In some legends, humans downstream get sick when La Madre Monte washes her hair in the river. In this way, people blame La Madre Monte for diseases, including both shingles and scabies. Other variations say storms and flooding follow whenever she bathes in the river. Stories like these use La Madre Monte to explain disease and dangerous weather before any understanding of germ theory or meteorology.

Like the mysterious Mapinguari (page 174), the beautiful La Madre Monte guards her area fiercely, embodying the green fecundity of a healthy forest. It is fitting that she gives her name to the Madre Monte preservation reserve in the Colombian Andes.

Yet some sources describe La Madre Monte as evil. In these tales, she draws walkers into the forest with her screams. This recasts her as an alluring, siren-like figure, speaking to a fear of both a powerful feminine goddess and the primal dangers of nature. The idea is simple: if we stay out of her domain, we have nothing to fear.

Resources

BOOKS

African & Caribbean Folktales, Myths & Legends – Wendy Shearer

American Indian Genesis: The Story of Creation – Percy Bullchild

American Indian Myths and Legends – Richard Erdoes and Alfonso Ortiz

The Book of Yokai: Mysterious Creatures of Japanese Folklore – Michael Dylan Foster

Breverton's Phantasmagoria: A Compendium of Monsters, Myths and Legends – Terry Breverton

Chinese Fairy Tales & Fantasies – Moss Roberts

Folktales from India – AK Ramanujan

Pagan Portals – Gods and Goddesses of Ireland: A Guide to Irish Deities – Morgan Daimler

Irish Fairy Tales and Folklore – W B Yeats

Islam, Arabs, and the Intelligent World of the Jinn – Amira El-Zein

The Jade Guidebook: A Visitor's Guide to Hell

Latin American Folktales: Stories from Hispanic and Indian Traditions – John Bierhorst

Love in Colour: Mythical Tales from Around the World – Bolu Babalola

Mythos: The Greek Myths Retold – Stephen Fry

Norse Gods – Johan Egerkrans

One Thousand and One Nights

Orishas, Goddesses, and Voodoo Queens: The Divine Feminine in the African Religious Traditions – Lilith Dorsey

The Runaway Princess and Other Stories – Helen Nde

Russian Fairy Tales – Alexander Afanasyev

Seven Sisters of the Pleiades: Stories from Around the World – Munya Andrews

Storyland: A New Mythology of Britain – Amy Jeffs

A Treasury of British Folklore: Maypoles, Mandrakes and Mistletoe – Dee Dee Chainey

Yiddish Folktales – Beatrice Weinreich

PODCASTS

Afro Tales

The Appalachian Folklore

The Asian Tapestry

By the Fire

Celtic Myths and Legends

The Faerie Folk

The Folklore Podcast

The Folk Tale Project

Ghosts and Folklore of Wales

Giraffe's Eggs And Other African Tales

The Hidden Djinn

Jewitches

Legendary Africa

Lore

Mythos

Spirit Box: Folklore, Magick & Spirits

Uncanny Japan

WEBSITES

A Book of Creatures – abookofcreatures.com
American Folklore – americanfolklore.net
American Folklore Society – americanfolkloresociety.org
Fairy Talez – fairytalez.com
Folklore Thursday – folklorethursday.com
Mythopedia – mythopedia.com
The Folklore Society – folklore-society.com
World of Tales – worldoftales.com

Pronunciation guide

Cailleach (Gaelic). Various acceptable pronunciations, including: Ky • och and Kay • och
'Och' should rhyme with 'loch'
Muma Pădurii (Romanian). Moo • ma Pa • dur • i
Cihuateteo (Mexican Spanish). Ci • wa • tay • tayo
La Llorona (Mexican Spanish). La Yo • ro • na
Tlazolteotl (Mexican Spanish). Tlah • zoh • tay • oht
The final 'L' is almost silent, just barely breathed
Papa Bois (French patois). Pa • pa Bwah
'Bwah' should rhyme with 'mwah'
La Diablesse (French patois). La Jah • bless
Sometimes spelled Ladjablès
Scheherazade (Arabic). Shuh • heh • ruh • zaad
Churel (Hindi; also appears in Urdu). Chuh • rail
Has several variant spellings, including Charail, Churreyl, Chudail, and Chudel
Taraka (Sanskrit). Taa • rah • ker
Variously spelled as Tataka, Tadaka, or Thataka
Mapinguari (Brazilian Portuguese). Mappin • gwar • i
Yemanja (Brazilian Portuguese). Ye • man • ja
Sometimes spelled Iemanja
Huayramama (Peruvian Spanish). Why • rah • mama

Index

189

About the author and illustrator

Icy Sedgwick is the host of the *Fabulous Folklore* podcast, investigating the strange and often bizarre world of European folklore (with a focus on the British Isles). She's particularly fascinated by the appearance of folklore in popular culture, but also the ways in which folklore preserves information in an easily transmissible format. In case she tires of all that folklore research, former ghost hunter Icy also writes Gothic horror fiction while studying for a PhD, looking at the representation of haunted houses in contemporary Hollywood cinema. Like any good folklorist, she has a horseshoe over her door, and she doesn't stray too close to bodies of water...

Melissa Kitty Jarram is a Southeast-London-based artist working across digital and traditional mediums for clients such as Bethany Williams, WePresent, Adidas, and Nike. She embraces not only the beauty, but the hardships of the female experience and the violence inherent in life through her illustrations, paintings, and moving image pieces. Her work is suffused with mythology—an extensive source of inspiration that, to this day, still unearths the depths of human nature and lends an invaluable insight into human psychology. Breaking 'the male gaze' is important to Jarram as she continues to explore and interpret the female form.

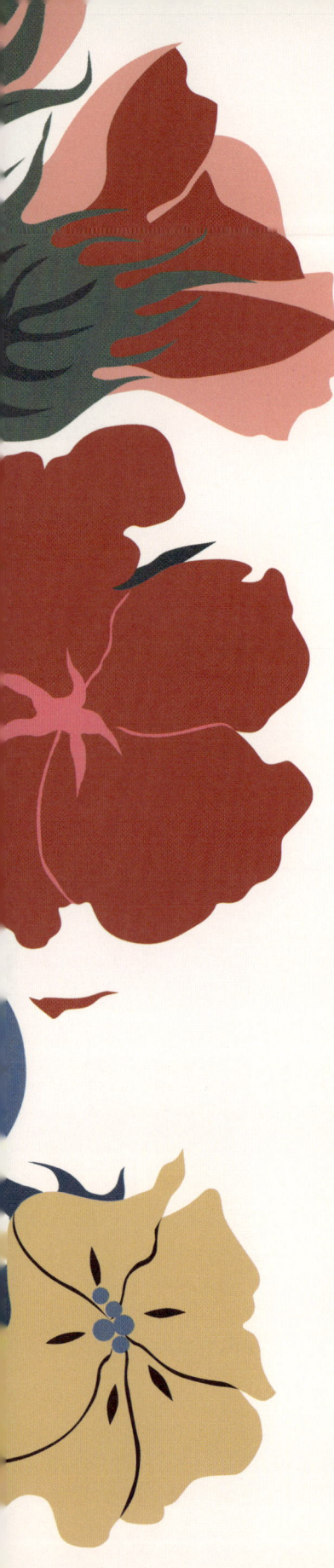

DK LONDON

Commissioning Editor Florence Ward
Senior Designer Lauren Adams
Managing Editor Pete Jorgensen
Managing Art Editor Jo Connor
Production Editor Siu Yin Chan
Production Controller Louise Minihane
Publisher Mark Searle

Art Director Giorgia Chiarion
Illustrator Melissa Kitty Jarram

DK would like to thank Tom Howells for proofreading
and Vanessa Bird for indexing. Thanks to Lang Shot Photography for the
photo of Icy Sedgwick and Rachel Manning for the photo of Melissa Jarram.

First American Edition, 2023
Published in the United States by DK Publishing
1745 Broadway, 20th Floor, New York, NY 10019

A catalog record for this book
is available from the Library of Congress.
ISBN 978-0-7440-8453-5

DK books are available at special discounts when purchased
in bulk for sales promotions, premiums, fund-raising, or educational use.
For details, contact: DK Publishing Special Markets,
1745 Broadway, 20th Floor, New York, NY 10019
SpecialSales@dk.com

Printed and bound in China

For the curious
www.dk.com

MIX
Paper | Supporting
responsible forestry
FSC™ C018179

This book was made with Forest
Stewardship Council™ certified
paper — one small step in DK's
commitment to a sustainable future.
For more information go to
www.dk.com/our-green-pledge